Your Horoscope 2023

....

Leo

23 July – 23 August

igloobooks

igloobooks

Published in 2022
First published in the UK by Igloo Books Ltd
An imprint of Igloo Books Ltd
Cottage Farm, NN6 0BJ, UK
Owned by Bonnier Books
Sveavägen 56, Stockholm, Sweden
www.igloobooks.com

0722 001
2 4 6 8 10 9 7 5 3 1
ISBN 978-1-80108-402-4

Written by Sally Kirkman
Additional content by Belinda Campbell and Denise Evans

Cover designed by Richard Sykes
Interiors designed by Chris Stanley
Edited by Luke Robertson

Printed and manufactured in China

CONTENTS

INTRODUCTION
· · · · · · · · · · · · · · · · ·

This 15-month guide has been designed and written to give
a concise and accessible insight into both the nature of your
star sign and the year ahead. Divided into two main sections,
the first part of this guide will give you an overview of your
character in order to help you understand how you think,
perceive the world and interact with others and – perhaps just
as importantly – why. You'll soon see that your zodiac sign
is not just affected by a few stars in the sky, but by planets,
elements and a whole host of other factors, too.

The second part of this guide is made up of daily forecasts.
Use these to increase your awareness of what might appear on
your horizon so that you're better equipped to deal with the
days ahead. While this should never be used to dictate your life,
it can be useful to see how your energies might be affected or
influenced, which in turn can help you prepare for what life
might throw your way.

By the end of these 15 months, these two sections should
have given you a deeper understanding and awareness of
yourself and, in turn, the world around you. There are never
any certainties in life, but with an open mind you will find
guidance for what might be, and learn to take more control of
your own destiny.

THE CHARACTER OF THE LION

· · · · · · · · · · · · · · · · · ·

A fire sign ruled by the Sun was surely always destined to burn the brightest. Like a moth to a flame, people are naturally drawn to Leonians. Whether singing on a stage, dancing in a club or playing football in the park, they dominate every situation by demanding attention and adoration. Born in the fifth house of the zodiac calendar, which represents pleasure and creativity, Leonians often derive immense satisfaction and a sense of purpose from making others happy. These fiery lions can be brimming with confidence or struggle with a lack thereof, and may need to be validated with constant praise. The laughter of others is like music to their ears, so a career in comedy, like fellow Leonians Jo Brand and Frankie Boyle, could prove to be their calling.

Born in the middle of summer, Leo is a fixed sign that works hard at making their dreams become a reality. Daring Leonians Amelia Earhart, Neil Armstrong and Barack Obama achieved historical firsts when realising their ambitions. Courageous and not averse to taking risks, fortune definitely favours the brave where Leonians are concerned: second place was not invented for these gold medal fans. Leonians can be competitive to a fault and sometimes need reminding that there is more to life than winning. At times they are exhausting to behold, but fortunately there is also plenty to love. What they lack in modesty, Leonians make up for in loyalty: they are known for being fiercely committed to loved ones and personal goals. At their best, these charismatic leaders rule with a generous heart and a visionary mind.

THE LION

It's hard to miss Leonians when they proudly stride into a room. These beings are the kings and queens of their jungle and expect to be received as such. Give Leonians the royal treatment and they'll soon be purring sweetly. However, contradict or disrespect them, and get ready to hear their roar. This sign is fierce but loyal: as true leaders of their pack, Leonians can be relied on to give guidance and do favours for their loved ones. Strength and courage usually typify the Leonian approach, but they also have a side as soft and beautiful as a lion's mane. The body part associated with Leo is the heart, and these Lions have big ones. Romance from Leonians will be dramatic and bold, so their lovers should expect to be serenaded in the street or proposed to via a message written in the sky. 'Go big or go home' is often the Leonian mantra, because they were not born to blend into the background.

THE SUN

The Sun sits at the centre of the universe, and those born under the sign of Leo naturally assume the same position. This makes them charismatic and popular, and, just like the Sun, their absence is felt on days when they are not around. Conversely, there are times when Leonians blaze too brightly, forcing those around them to seek shade! However, Leonians can heal just as they can hurt: Apollo is one of the Greek gods of the Sun, recognised in part for his ability to heal and protect. Apollo was also associated with music and the arts, and this may explain why this Sun-led sign is drawn to taking centre stage. Whether they pursue a creative career in the arts or not, the Sun's influence means Leonians usually have a strong sense of who they are and where they are going in life.

ELEMENTS, MODES AND POLARITIES

Each sign is made up of a unique combination of three defining groups: elements, modes and polarities. Each of these defining parts can manifest themselves in good and bad ways and none should be seen as a positive or a negative – including the polarities! Just like a jigsaw puzzle, piecing these groups together can help illuminate why each sign has certain characteristics and help us find a balance.

ELEMENTS

Fire: Dynamic and adventurous, signs with fire in them are often extroverted. Others are naturally drawn to them because of the positive light they give off, as well as their high levels of energy and confidence.

Earth: Signs with the earth element are steady and driven by their ambitions. They make for solid friends, parents or partners due to their grounded influence and nurturing nature.

Air: The invisible element that influences each of the other elements significantly, air signs provide much-needed perspective to those around them with their fair thinking, verbal skills and key ideas.

Water: Warm in the shallows but sometimes as freezing as ice, this mysterious element is essential to the growth of everything around it, through its emotional depth and empathy.

MODES

Cardinal: Pioneers of the calendar, cardinal signs jump-start each season and are the energetic go-getters.

Fixed: Marking the middle of the calendar, fixed signs firmly denote and value both steadiness and reliability.

Mutable: As the seasons end, the mutable signs adapt and gladly give themselves over to the promise of change.

POLARITIES

Positive: Typically extroverted, positive signs take physical action and embrace outside stimulus in their life.

Negative: Usually introverted, negative signs value emotional development and experiencing life from the inside out.

LEO IN BRIEF

The table below shows the key attributes of Leonians. Use it for quick reference and to understand more about this fascinating sign.

SYMBOL	RULING PLANET	MODE	ELEMENT	HOUSE
♌	☉	⊟	△	♊
The Lion	The Sun	Fixed	Fire	Fifth

COLOURS	BODY PARTS	POLARITY	GENDER	POLAR SIGN
		⊕	♂	≋
Purple, Gold	Heart and Spine	Positive	Masculine	Aquarius

ROMANTIC RELATIONSHIPS

. . . .

Leonians are associated with the heart, which is perhaps why they love being in love. They take great pleasure in moving heaven and Earth to romance the socks off their love interests. Whether it's a Bridget Jones-style kiss in the snow or even standing at the front of a ship like Jack and Rose, these brave Lions will romance their partners as effectively as any romcom movie character. Whether such bold statements of love appeal is a question of personal taste, but it's difficult not to fall head over heels for these charismatic charmers.

Leonians are the performers of the calendar and have no problem having admiring eyes on them. Throw roses at their feet and they will provide an encore; clap too enthusiastically, however, and the Leonian ego may take over. They appreciate partners that shower them with praise, but they should try not to demand it. Practising modesty and channelling a quieter confidence can make Leonians even more charming.

Although Leonians' demands in love can be great, they will give themselves wholeheartedly to their partners. No expense will be spared in their generous gestures of romance, but it will be their staggering displays of loyalty that will probably be appreciated the most. Once they have set their sights on someone, they will be honest and faithful until the end. Leonians have a fearless approach to love, which means that they open themselves up to plenty of heartbreak. Their courage, however, is contagious, and their willingness to take risks can lead to the biggest rewards in love.

ARIES: COMPATIBILITY 2/5

Arians are used to being first, but they'll have to learn to
share the spotlight and responsibility for decision-making
if they fall for a leader of the jungle. These two signs should
recognise their similarities and know just how to support one
another in reaching their goals. With the Leonian led by the
heart and the Arian by the head, arguments can be a roaring
battle when these two don't see eye to eye. Ego and pride will
need to be kept in check on both sides if this relationship is to
go the distance.

TAURUS: COMPATIBILITY 3/5

Leo is ruled by the Sun and Taurus by Venus, a star and planet
that are never further than 48 degrees from each other. The
love that these two share is solidified in their sometimes-
stubborn commitment to one another. The Lion and Bull are
both fixed signs, and this can be their undoing in a long-term
relationship, especially when neither is willing to compromise.
Both the Lion and Bull will shower each other with affection
and admiration, and should boost each other's self-esteem.
However, this couple should be careful not to let their egos get
in the way of their shared happiness.

GEMINI: COMPATIBILITY 4/5

The inner Leonian child might be just what the youthful sign of Gemini asked for. This pairing can be like a children's story full of love and adventure: think Peter Pan and Wendy. The high-energy Leonian was born to lead, while the mutable Geminian is happy to take the Lion's hand and fly speedily off to Neverland! The Leonian will encourage the Geminian to take an active part in the important choices in their lives. Both are positive signs, and their extrovert energies and curious natures will see this air and fire match embark on endless adventures.

CANCER: COMPATIBILITY 1/5

Leo is ruled by the Sun and Cancer by the moon, so this pairing can feel as different as night and day. However, the Lion and the Crab may also find that they have plenty in common, and should be able to form a lasting love. Born in the fourth and fifth houses that partly signify family and children, the Leonian and Cancerian share a fundamental desire to find a long-term partner to settle down with. Security is essential for the Cancerian, and the fixed side of the steadfast Leonian can provide just that. This power couple could go the distance if their differences are embraced.

LEO: COMPATIBILITY 3/5

When a Leonian loves a Leonian, it's like stars colliding and causing a supernova. Beautiful and dramatic, these two creatives are naturally pulled together. Many Leonians use their talents for the dramatics in the arts, so this fiery partnership could spark on the set of a movie or in some other creative industry; actors Ben Affleck and Jennifer Lopez are a prime example of this. However, like with Affleck and Lopez, a long future together is not always guaranteed. While the fun and romance will be plentiful, these two fixed signs may struggle to cooperate.

VIRGO: COMPATIBILITY 2/5

The love of a Leonian can take a Virgoan by surprise, which isn't something the introverted Virgoan is always keen on. The clear differences between the studious Virgoan and showstopping Leonian might mean that these two are quick to write each other off as potential partners. The relationship between this fire and earth couple can be a slow burner, but their steady approach might mean these two win the race hand in hand. This couple's strength is their differences, and these hard workers can make for a solid and complementary pairing.

LIBRA: COMPATIBILITY 4/5

Sitting two places apart on the calendar, a Libran and Leonian should make for a compatible partnership. The Libran is an expert in diplomacy, so will likely be able to handle the more dramatic moments of this love affair without bruising the Leonian's ego. Love with the Leonian can be a roller coaster, both fun and full of ups and downs. The Libran, symbolised by scales, will try to bring a balance to the relationship that the reliable Leonian will appreciate. Ruled by the Sun and Venus, the Leonian and Libran are capable of forming a relationship that is full of warmth and love.

SCORPIO: COMPATIBILITY 1/5

The love between watery Scorpio and fiery Leo can be one of deep intimacy or dampened spirits. These are two fixed signs that may clash in their different approaches, refusing to yield to each other's strong personalities. Shared assets, particularly money, could prove difficult for them, as Scorpio is born in the eighth house where shared possessions are important, while Leo belongs in the fifth house where love and pleasure are highlighted. This contract could result in serious conflict for the couple, but if respect is exercised regularly between these two lovers, theirs is a closeness well worth protecting.

SAGITTARIUS: COMPATIBILITY 4/5

This fire sign match will surely spark with excitement. This is a pairing in which both partners are likely to plan a surprise romantic getaway for the other with little or no notice. Both are spontaneous and adventurous, and the Leonian and Sagittarian match each other with their positive energies. They are likely to be the dynamic couple at the top of every party invite list. It's not all about glittering events, though, and the philosophical Sagittarian and purpose-led Leonian can share a powerful bond, with an influence that is felt beyond just the two of them.

CAPRICORN: COMPATIBILITY 4/5

A Leonian and Capricornian can tell a successful love story in which opposites attract. Both tend to share a clear sense of purpose; for the Leonian, it's their personal life that drives them, and for the Capricornian, it's their career. Leonian Barack Obama and Capricornian Michelle Obama are an ideal example of how well these two can work towards achieving their dreams together. The Capricornian can show the Leonian the benefits of hard work, while the Leonian can bring the fun that sometimes the cool and dignified Capricornian is sometimes lacking. These are two very strong characters that can be even stronger together.

AQUARIUS: COMPATIBILITY 5/5

Aquarius is the air sign that sparks the embers of Leo's fire element into a full blaze. Opposites on the calendar, this combination of shared positive energy, fixed attitudes and complementary elements makes for a couple that were astrologically meant to be. These unique characters can be guilty of feeling superior to others, so may need be reminded to treat each other as equals. This is often a partnership sprung from fun and crafted by a shared creativity. The visionary mind of the Leonian combined with the Aquarian's ideals could see these two creating a utopian life together.

PISCES: COMPATIBILITY 2/5

When a Leonian meets a Piscean, they can bring out the best and worst in each other. The Piscean can be a source of emotional encouragement for the Leonian, while the Leonian might help the dreamy Piscean take more action to fully realise their dreams. Born in the twelfth house, which represents sacrifice, the Piscean is often selfless, while the Sun-ruled Leonian can be the opposite. When these two opposing characteristics are felt at their extremes, this relationship can turn toxic. However, the mutable Piscean and fixed Leonian can live in harmony if they are able to value each other's best qualities.

FAMILY AND FRIENDS

All great leaders have a loyal following of subjects, and intrepid Leonians are no exception. Like the Sun, they have the power to draw their friends and families outside to spend time in their warm embrace. Being around heartfelt Lions can lift people's spirits and provide huge amounts of fun and joy. Their outgoing and extroverted energy is contagious, but it can also be tiring. Fellow positive signs make for great high-energy friends that can easily keep up with these social butterflies. More introverted negative signs can also play an important role, as a Leonian will appreciate a friend or family member for whom they don't have to constantly put on a performance. These people offer an important change of pace and an opportunity to recharge.

All the love and support that Leonians receive from their family and friends, will be returned threefold, as this sign is most known for its unparalleled generosity. Leonians love luxury, so their gifts are often extravagant, whether they have the cash to spoil their loved ones or not. If their bank accounts aren't quite big enough to indulge their friends, Leonians can be creative with even the smallest of budgets. Leonians will share money if they have it but, more importantly, they will always give their valued time and energy to those around them.

Belonging to the fifth house in the calendar, which is closely associated with children, the protective and high-spirited Leonian can be a wonderful and empathetic parent. In some ways, Leonians never grow up, so more vividly remember the frustrations of being young. Their inner child will bring the fun and energy required when raising offspring, or they will be the fun aunt or uncle that their nieces and nephews always want to play with. If Leonians don't have children of their own, other people's will no doubt gravitate towards them. This often means Leonians are happy to be the go-to babysitter or first choice to be a godparent.

While sunny Leonians can have a warm and healing quality, their stage-hogging presence can be overpowering and destructive in their relationships. Their roar is as loud as a lion's, and risks drowning out everyone else. It may not be the intention of Leonians to overshadow their friends and family, but the influence of their guiding Sun can turn this confident ruler into a bossy dictator. Their fixed attitudes can make them resistant to the opinions of others, but Leonians should avoid surrounding themselves with people that agree with them. A diverse social network where everyone has a voice is the only kingdom worthy of Leonian leadership.

MONEY AND CAREERS

. . . .

Being a particular star sign will not dictate that you follow a certain type of career, but it can help you to identify potential areas to thrive in. Conversely, to succeed in the workplace, it is just as important to understand your strengths and weaknesses to achieve career and financial goals.

Their aristocratic tendencies and love of luxury creates a risk that Leonians can become too focused on the material things in life. It can be good to enjoy the finer things in life, as long as doing so doesn't dominate everything. However, if Leonians can channel their love for grand things creatively, they might follow in the footsteps of notable Leonian fashion designers such as Yves Saint-Laurent, Coco Chanel and Michael Kors. Rather than wearing the designer names of others, Leonians possess a passion for luxury and leadership that could help them become the next big name that everyone covets.

While Leonians enjoy the best in life, they will generally be sensible with their finances and not spend beyond their means. An unexpected trip might be tempting, but they aren't usually the type to go for broke and risk losing it all. The fixed part of Leonians will keep their spending steady, as they are unwilling to risk losing their financial security. They may be driven to earn lots of money so that they can buy all the luxuries they desire, but they will probably earn their fortune through organised efforts and a steadfast approach rather than at the slot machines.

Whether Leonians go for the leading roles in a film or strive to lead a country, they will be comfortable in the spotlight of their choosing. Leonians' natural self-assurance makes them authoritative and confident figures, and others will respect that. Whether it's the moves of Leonian Mick Jagger, the skills of Harry Kane or the leadership of Barack Obama, all eyes will be firmly on them.

If fame doesn't appeal to a Leonian, managerial roles could be their natural domain, while occupations in the world of luxury are also appealing given Leonians' appreciation of the finer things in life. No matter the field, being in charge is often the primary goal, although a bossy attitude should be avoided wherever possible to keep others happy.

As with family, colleagues cannot be chosen. It can therefore be advantageous to use star signs to learn about their key characteristics and discover the best ways of working together. Part of the attraction for becoming a leader for Leonians is the thrill of competition; the king or queen of the jungle loves to demonstrate their prowess by rising above any competitors. However, dominating Leonians may need to remind themselves that there is no 'I' in 'team', especially if they are working with similarly minded characters, such as Arians. Taureans might share the same ambitious dreams as Leonians, but any colleague that is also a fixed sign will need to work harder at finding a place to compromise.

HEALTH AND WELLBEING

. . . .

These bold Lions can also be highly sensitive souls. Like anyone, they have their ups and downs, so friends and family can be the essential supporters that straighten the crown on their ruler's head. The critical words of Virgoans might be felt too harshly by sensitive Leonians and can knock their confidence if they are feeling low. Pisceans and Cancerians should tread more carefully and be emotionally encouraging friends that help Leonians stride forward again. A need for constant reassurance can stem from a crisis of confidence, so Leonians should work on building up their own self-esteem from within to avoid the need to rely on others to lift them out of their low moods. Owning their mistakes and recognising where they can improve are just a couple of ways that Leonians can grow to become happier and humbler.

Winning can feel wonderful, but when Leonians reach their desired peak, they may find themselves at a loss. Once Leonians rise to the top of their profession, they may need to take up another hobby or avenue of interest to satisfy their urge to win. Throwing themselves into a competitive sport that takes them outside will appease their ambitious side, provide youthful energy and remind them of their love of the Sun. While protection from harmful UV rays is important, spending time in the Sun sensibly can be just as vital for keeping healthy. Apart from providing essential Vitamin D, sunshine's healing properties also lower cholesterol and reduce high blood pressure – wonderful news for heart-associated Leonians. Learning lines for their latest play in the sunshine or swimming in a lido rather than an indoor swimming pool could also improve physical and mental health.

· · · · · · · · · · · · · · · · ·

Guided by the Sun, which represents the self and life's purpose, onlookers will assume that Leonians know who they are and where they are going. If Leonians lack direction in life, it can be a major source of upset for them, especially if they feel that they aren't living up to their own expectations or the expectations of others. Leonians should try to take the pressure off themselves and understand that learning who they truly are and where they wish to get to in life are two big issues that plague everyone. They would do well to cut themselves some slack and not get bogged down by their reputation of always being the best. The high status of the charismatic, larger-than-life Lion can be a burden to Leonians that feel they don't fit the bill. They are the best at being themselves, so should not attempt to cage themselves within the confines of expectation.

Leo

. . . .

DAILY FORECASTS
for 2022

OCTOBER

. . . .

Saturday 1st

Try not to barge through a partner's boundaries today. It's likely that you're feeling optimistic and joyful, but remember that your significant other might not feel the same way. This contrast can make it difficult to feel closeness, so you may need to be flexible and accommodating until they're ready to join in with your joy.

Sunday 2nd

Mercury turns direct now, so you may find that the fog begins to lift from your true north. However, you must be cautious, as there may still be an illusion underneath. There's little point starting something new today, as the energy suggests that you could lose interest very quickly.

Monday 3rd

Watch out for opportunities at work to enhance your finances or make more sense of your personal growth. Offers from earlier in the year may be up for review. Is there anything you can do to tailor an experience to suit you better? Can you put your own spin on things?

Tuesday 4th

You would be wise to use practical skills to ensure you get noticed this morning. As the day progresses, so will your visibility to those who matter. Mental activity may take over, so you might be networking or gathering resources and allies for an exciting future project.

Wednesday 5th

You may feel a little stuck today, but there's a chance you can work around this by thinking outside the box. Be prepared to take the advice of others on board. Don't dismiss anything until you've had time to see if it could work for you.

Thursday 6th

Merging with like-minded people and getting lost in love can take you to ethereal and magical places, but you will need to keep one foot on planet Earth today, or you might succumb to temptation. It's a good time to combine forces and upgrade your relationships instead of fighting from opposite corners.

Friday 7th

Listen to your inner voice today, as it may tell you what needs to be released or transformed in order for you to grow. You might receive a lesson in starting at the beginning and not jumping straight into the middle. Your intuition will guide you, so stay alert for subliminal messages and signposts.

Saturday 8th

You could feel pulled in directions that don't feel safe or real today, so hold onto your true north and let it be your anchor. Don't do anything rash now, as things may get out of hand and return to bite you. Make sure that any new plans for travel are realistic and sensible.

Sunday 9th

A full moon can throw the spotlight on your travel and education plans. You might reflect on your actions over the last six months, especially if something comes to fruition now. Pluto turns direct and may bring with it an ending concerning mundane work duties.

Monday 10th

You should feel more outgoing today and may wish that you'd taken up invitations at the weekend. This might mean that you now want to play catch up with your social network. Be your best self in the workplace, as your leadership skills may be needed to organise new projects or to discard old ones.

Tuesday 11th

Negotiation could become a theme for you in the next few weeks. This may come naturally to you, especially if you can converse with a persuasive style. You might recall skills you have learnt to help you get your own way, but it's also important to listen.

Wednesday 12th

The tricky planetary energy may give you a rollercoaster of a day; you might think you're winning one minute and see it all fall apart the next. Deal with this by removing any expectations for outcomes beyond your control. Changes will come whether you want them to or not, so be practical and stay grounded.

Thursday 13th

You may wish to seek advice from your close friends and groups today, and there might be someone who has wisdom to share. If an issue stops you in your tracks, try to listen to the whole story, not just one side.

Friday 14th

You should find that you have more time for others today, especially if you're feeling unusually altruistic and patient. A good cause may have touched a soft spot, leading you to offer your services. Know your place and learn all about it before committing on a whim.

Saturday 15th

You have a choice to make this weekend: you can either retreat and be alone with your thoughts, or you can be defensive on behalf of others. You may also feel part of something big and wish to add your voice to a caring and nurturing cause.

Sunday 16th

If your emotions are activated, ensure they are in sync with your mind. Try not to be over-sensitive about something that you haven't fully thought through. Make sure that you have all the facts before making an emotional decision, or you may find that you need to undo things at a later date.

Monday 17th

You may become entangled in a web of misunderstanding today. Even if you think you're doing the right thing, you might feel manipulated or coerced. Try not to commit to anything that will become a burden. If you can get out of something, do so politely.

Tuesday 18th

The moon drops into your sign today, so you should be able to find your voice. You may be shouting about recent events or making a scene, but try not to get above yourself now. If there's an injustice against you specifically, feel free to question it.

Wednesday 19th

If you need to make waves today, draw on the archetype of the compassionate warrior and realise that there are ways of dealing with unrest that don't require aggression. Be respectful and assertive.

Thursday 20th

A struggle for control may surface, but today's energy suggests that, with proper management and strategy, you can handle it. If you keep emotions out of your decision-making, you may get somewhere.

Friday 21st

Today you should look at what holds value for you. What can you not do without? Decide what is worth holding onto and what has been holding you back. This also includes family relationships and work issues. Have a think about what makes you feel good or bad.

Saturday 22nd

There could be a last-minute thing to do concerning messaging or visiting in your locality. It may be better to get this done in the morning before you get bogged down with other obligations. A day of practical activity should take your mind off other worries and things that aren't sitting well.

Sunday 23rd

Saturn turns direct today, so you might be reviewing the subject of boundaries and limits regarding your significant relationship. If this has been an issue for you this year, try to come to an understanding now. Love and seduction may become a theme, so long as you are both comfortable.

Monday 24th

You might find that partnerships are on the mend now, especially if you've developed more trust. When there's a good balance in a relationship, things can be discussed calmly and equally. Your head and heart are likely to be in sync, which will aid any deep discussions.

Tuesday 25th

A new moon and a solar eclipse open a window of wildcard energy today, so anything can happen. It's possible that you see issues of jealousy or power struggles arising within your family; however, you should have the ability and compassion to handle this well.

Wednesday 26th

Try not to resurrect old issues from the past when dealing with family, as things may implode and become detrimental to your day. Remember what you've learned from Saturn this year and maintain healthy and loving boundaries. Your patience may be tested, but you could win the respect of those around you if you bring about a happy resolution.

. . . .

Thursday 27th

Use your intelligence before becoming emotional today. You might have more luck making changes and setting ground rules if you are guided by logic and reason. You may take off and soar to higher levels in your romance and creative pursuits this afternoon. Make the most of this energy.

Friday 28th

You and a partner or a group of friends may revisit an experience that was fathomless and spiritual, and you could once again be on cloud nine. Make sure that this isn't anything superficial, and keep it real by anchoring yourself to your love.

Saturday 29th

If you wake up feeling drained, it might be best to stay cosy and quiet with a loved one. Shared duties and intense conversations could bring the two of you even closer together. Cooking, eating or doing mundane chores can be a delight if you have someone to share them with. Prepare for conversations to get juicy.

Sunday 30th

Mars turns retrograde today, and this may herald a time of turbulence and blocks within friendship groups. Social interactions might reach a stalemate situation. However, for today, try to enjoy a time of sweet mystery and depth.

Monday 31st

Stay in control of your feelings today, especially if the working week dampens your good spirits. Don't be tempted to raise a revolution, even if there are cross words within your family that risk getting nasty. Rise above it and be respectful and mature, as this will likely pass and be forgotten about soon.

NOVEMBER

. . . .

Tuesday 1st
You may be presented with several challenges that bring out your shadow side today. If you feel on edge, you might find that any little thing triggers an adverse reaction. Understand that this is temporary. Resolve to keep a low profile, and don't provoke an argument that you won't win.

Wednesday 2nd
Take things slowly today, especially if your mental energy is overloaded or blocked. There might be confusion or aggression within your friendship groups and close relationships. This evening will be lighter if you stay adaptable and are willing to let go of any grievances. It's time to heal old wounds.

Thursday 3rd
Your sense of empathy is likely to be strengthened now, and this will help if you're fixing problems with family members. Humble yourself and apologise where necessary. Try to enter into negotiations with more compassion, as doing so will help you feel connected not only by blood but also by love and spirit. Merging with your soul group can be soothing.

Friday 4th
A change of direction is often uncomfortable, but you should realise that it will feel right for you eventually. Issues within your social groups need to be avoided, not antagonised. Serving others with unconditional love can fill your heart and bring you more joy and optimism.

Saturday 5th

You're likely to feel more outgoing and have more passion for your dreams and intentions today, and this means that you will see clearly where you have been held back by certain karmic connections. Consider cutting these ties suddenly and with total conviction.

Sunday 6th

A conflict may arise that is simply about spending time with a lover or friends. Choose wisely, as you may resent your time being wasted by either party. Your inner voice will remind you of what you've let go of recently, but will also give you encouragement and the confidence to move on.

Monday 7th

You might be in a better mood today, although you could also be a little stubborn. Small annoyances with family and lovers may test your patience, so you will need to remember your personal boundaries. Try to balance your home life with the work you do in the wider world.

Tuesday 8th

A full moon and a lunar eclipse often show the closure of a recent episode, so a project may be completed and ready to move to the next level now. There's anticipation in the air, so you might find it hard to stay still and keep quiet. Something wonderful is ready to burst into life.

. . . .

Wednesday 9th

You may be very sociable today, but could also be at risk of revealing a secret or speaking too soon. Tread carefully today, especially if there's a lot depending on a certain issue. You may need to hold your tongue a little longer, which could prove to be tricky.

Thursday 10th

Be cautious and know your limits. If this is a crucial time, you don't want to spoil it by being reckless. A big dream may be coming true, so make sure the bubble doesn't burst. If your emotions are intense, remember that they can be shared.

Friday 11th

It might be tricky to follow your head today, especially if you're emotionally invested in doing the right thing. You may be dragged into something that goes against your core values. If things don't seem fair or just to you, walk away.

Saturday 12th

Consider spending time alone to nurture yourself with whatever makes you feel good. Great company can be soothing and remind you that you're loved. Listen to your intuition today, especially if there are mysteries that are unravelling. Don't let anyone fool you with false promises.

Sunday 13th

You might be building your comfort zone around you and inviting those who you feel safe with to come inside. These people are likely to be on your wavelength. Enjoy the emotions you feel today and let them guide you towards a better course.

Monday 14th

Stay in control and try not to react if someone pushes your buttons today. If you experience a small trigger, try to deal with it admirably. It should be safe to emerge and let your voice be heard this afternoon. Shine your light and attract others to it.

Tuesday 15th

An act of compassion can go a long way. Your family may need reassurance or advice, and you could be the one to deal with any communication or enquiries. Money matters might come to a head and need your attention.

Wednesday 16th

Fight for your rights today, but remember to do so with total honesty. Look out for any false dealings that could damage you or your family, such as a trickster or some energy that is elusive and unclear. Try to uncover any falsehoods and see the truth behind the lies.

Thursday 17th

Check all the facts today, then check them again. This is a good day to go through your paperwork and finances. Mercury joins Venus in your romantic and creative zone, and this means that you should be able to be more articulate with words of love.

Friday 18th

Restlessness could be the fuel you need to get your work done today. You might be fine-tuning some details and using radical methods to solve problems. A focus on practical work might see you get things done in record time. Avoid any conflict or slow progress within your social groups.

Saturday 19th

Today you should have a sense that all is well in the world. Try to separate yourself from the problems of others and concentrate on what means the most to you. A healthy regard for a romantic partner will inspire you to create beautiful things and have heartfelt conversations.

Sunday 20th

Your mind is likely to be busy processing a lot of ideas that pertain to your love relationship. An understanding might have been reached that is both respectful and mature, perhaps involving a better sense of boundaries and limits. Resolve to keep these boundaries in place to protect what you have with someone you love.

Monday 21st

You might need to add a finishing touch to something within your family group. This could involve some difficult emotions, especially if you're letting something go. Let those closest to you know that you're there to share this moment with them. Your love life might be filled with blessings this evening.

Tuesday 22nd

The Sun enters your romance and creative zone, so expect to be inspired to find your muse: your greatest work could be born from this energy. Expressing yourself should be easy now, as you will feel more able to speak your divine truth and search for the meaning of life.

Wednesday 23rd

Your emotions may be bigger than usual, so you may find that you're making grand gestures in several parts of your life. You might be skipping through your day feeling full of joy and optimism for the future. Enjoy the remarkable energy, but be careful not to overstretch yourself.

Thursday 24th

This is a wonderful day, so take note of what occurs. A new moon asks you to set goals and intentions regarding romance, creativity and your search for truth. Meanwhile, love is in the air, and your heart should be totally in sync with your head.

Friday 25th

Don't let anyone knock you from your happy place, even if you need to deal a difficult person who tries to put a downer on your day. It might be that this person simply dislikes another someone enjoying any fortune and happiness. Deal with them respectfully and compassionately.

Saturday 26th

Simple pleasures can sometimes bring the biggest smiles. Today you might feel that everything is where it should be and acknowledge that you've worked hard on self-improvement this year. Get your chores done, then do something just for you or share something with a close friend or lover.

Sunday 27th

It may become clear to you that your true north has moved away from where it once was, and that what was once important no longer is. Your experiences and fortunes this year are likely to have shifted your value system, so you may be looking at a healthier, less cluttered path.

Monday 28th

You might now be more open to helping a cause or doing good work in your community. Look for ways to make positive change happen with a new group of like-minded people. Try to entice your other social groups to get on board and participate.

Tuesday 29th

A partner may need all of your mental attention now. You may be bouncing through your day, especially if thoughts of love and closeness spur you on. Remember to come back down to earth and get your regular chores done. Stay away from argumentative or antagonistic groups this evening.

Wednesday 30th

Keep a grip on reality and try not to drift off to a fantasy island.
Consider the depths you will go to for someone you love,
and whether they would do the same. If you mean to share
everything with them, make sure that the feeling is mutual.
Do this through honest, open and loving communication.

DECEMBER

. . . .

Thursday 1st

It's possible that you could hit a snag and feel coerced into
something you don't wish to do today. If it feels wrong and not
in alignment with your best interests, walk away from it; this
is your inner compass keeping you on the straight and narrow.
Consider staying closer to home for now.

Friday 2nd

A keen sense of what is right and just will help you avoid any
unnecessary conflict. A partner may offer the support you
need, especially if you're feeling unsure about something. Set
your sights on whatever brings you security, even if this means
ignoring the impulse to go off on your own path.

Saturday 3rd

Steering your own boat may feel lonely, but if you know
what's good for you, your course will be true. Stay respectful
and responsible at all times, and put your energy into
whatever you feel passionate about. Try to ignore anyone who
tries to draft you to their cause.

Sunday 4th

Neptune turns direct now, so your inner compass should be
strong enough to pull you away from any potential trouble.
Listen to your inner voice and do practical work to distract
yourself from making any impulsive decisions. Stay grounded
and keep your mind busy with jobs around your home.

Monday 5th

If you need to shake things up a little today, then do so. This could relate to something has been dormant and has gathered dust, or a work issue that is yet to reach a breakthrough moment. You may also feel an urge to merge or connect with something bigger than yourself.

Tuesday 6th

You might need another push to finish a creative project or to let someone know how you feel. Put down roots and build solid foundations today, but understand that you can only do this by speaking honestly and staying true to your personal path. You should soon know the steps you need to take.

Wednesday 7th

Use today to gather your thoughts and resources. Thinking time will do you good and help you to process recent events. Like-minded friends can be encouraging and may offer you advice. Cover all your options.

Thursday 8th

What has come to light within your groups? Something may have been exposed, or you might experience aggressive behaviour. Alternatively, you may have reached a stalemate situation and be at a loss about how to move on. Explore all open avenues, but don't try to tear down brick walls.

Friday 9th

Retreat into your private zone and allow yourself to feel safe today. If life is uncertain, it might be best to be around those who love you unconditionally. If you feel sensitive to criticism, try not to engage or react negatively. Filter your words before speaking them aloud.

Saturday 10th

Stay safe now, especially if you're not in the right frame of mind to deal with any upsets. Look after your body by eating well. Choose the right company to make you feel more nurtured and protected, as you may experience a trigger that opens an old wound. Take the time to heal.

Sunday 11th

Your dreams will tell you where you should be heading, but you might still feel insecure and vulnerable, especially if things are moving quicker than you would like. This is likely to be a passing phase that is triggering your deepest self. Wait until you have more clarity.

Monday 12th

The moon is back in your sign today, so you should feel more like yourself again. You might be stirred up with passion and feel ready for action. Take this time to pause and reflect before making any moves. Surveying your territory will help you gauge the audience you need to convince.

Tuesday 13th

Be careful that you don't project your shadow side onto a partner. You may find that the strength of your convictions overwhelms you and that you need an outlet now. Try to use your creativity and self-expression to illustrate how you feel. Be open to any inspiration you receive.

Wednesday 14th

Get down to the nitty-gritty of the working day. Lists, plans and a clear out will all help you to focus. You should also check your health and consider starting a new exercise regime. This may feel like an arduous task, but it will ultimately have positive results.

Thursday 15th

Great earth energy should ensure that you get all your jobs done if you are more methodical and self-disciplined now. Avoid any distractions from social groups, as they're not likely to bring you much joy today. Happiness comes from ticking things off your list and clearing space for new things to come.

Friday 16th

Apply yourself to the job at hand and stay open to any changes you may need to make along the way. By the evening, you should feel satisfied by the knowledge that you've been productive and useful. Your dreams and visions might call, but they will need to wait for another time.

Saturday 17th

Find the time to take care of your own needs. This may mean starting a new exercise routine or planning a tasty evening meal that includes a love partner. Food, company and conversation are the themes of the day.

Sunday 18th

You may be tempted to chat the day away, but doing so will leave you feeling guilty. A lover may have something to discuss, but they should also encourage you to work first and play later. This evening is a good time for a lively conversation between the two of you.

Monday 19th

It's a good idea to be sincere in the workplace now. Try to find a way of offering your services that doesn't overwhelm you with more duties. Family matters can be intense, especially as the festive season approaches. You might need to make a plan or delegate jobs to ensure that all hands are on deck.

Tuesday 20th

Jupiter returns for a long stay in your travel zone. This is great news as it means that any holidays or interest in other cultures will likely take you far and wide. Try to be flexible and listen to your partner's views as you make plans together.

Wednesday 21st

The winter solstice arrives today and brings with it a long, dark night. This is perfect to snuggle down with a partner and express gratitude for the year gone by. Try to reflect on your personal growth and notice how far you've come. Set wheels in motion for some exploration in the new year.

Thursday 22nd

You might find that you wish to do something unusual now. An urge for pleasure, unplanned journeys and a taste of your dreams may fill you. Consider doing something outside the box. Find exciting new ways to have fun.

Friday 23rd

There's a new moon this morning, signalling the first step of a long inner journey. You may take stock of this and think that it's too big for you, but remember that you need to follow the rules and do things by the book to get where you want to be.

Saturday 24th

Love, merriment and great conversation will fill your heart today. Envision yourself walking side by side with the partner of your dreams on the long road to the realisation of your visions and ambitions. If you're planning for a future alone, take into consideration how this path looks to you.

Sunday 25th

Today is best spent with a partner, especially if you feel that your emotions are already focused on them. Think about the wider world and your small part in the global community: it may be time to offer your services to a good cause and contribute in some way.

Monday 26th

You might be tired and lacking in energy, but there are still likely to be family obligations to fulfil. The best thing to do today is be friendly and civil to others as you do your duties. Let everyone know where your limit is, especially if you overdid the good things yesterday.

. . . .

Tuesday 27th

Let yourself merge with the people closest to you and switch off for a while. You may want to indulge in more food and drink or simply relax. If you're on cloud nine, try to keep one foot on the ground and anchor yourself in reality. Everything should feel good and peaceful now.

Wednesday 28th

Keep an eye out for any blessings today, as they might come in an unexpected form. Your inner compass is in your grasp, and this may be intoxicating, especially if you feel that you're in an ethereal world where all your dreams will come true. Keep it real and don't get swept away.

Thursday 29th

Before the year ends, Mercury turns retrograde. Prepare for this by backing up all your devices and double-checking any travel plans. You might notice this influence immediately if plans for health or beauty are disturbed. Be mindful of conversations with a loved one, especially if there is a misunderstanding. Patience is key.

Friday 30th

A quiet day would be good for you now. You might be missing your friendship groups and want to get out and about, but there may not be much to join in with. It's a good time to think about plans for holidays and adventures in the coming year.

Saturday 31st

If you still don't have your New Year celebrations planned, consider staying at home and hosting them there. You may feel better if you are in control of the proceedings and the star of your own show. See out the old year in style by sharing your joy and optimism with the people you love most. Have a wonderful close to 2022.

Leo

....

DAILY FORECASTS
for 2023

JANUARY

. . . .

Sunday 1st
As 2023 begins, your thoughts may turn to your career. If
you've been having issues with a boss or colleague, you might
be keen to change your role when you go back to work. Make a
cosmic wish list for what you want to come next.

Monday 2nd
You may not be in the best place to make a clear decision
about your work or your health right now. A turning point
could come later this month, around the 18th. Until then,
explore your options and do your research, especially if you're
looking for a job or want to revitalise your energy.

Tuesday 3rd
Love planet Venus enters your relationship zone today. This
may have a strong influence on your love life and could bring
some much-needed heart into a relationship. It should be
easier to get on with other people over the next few weeks. If in
doubt, lead by example.

Wednesday 4th
Being loving and giving will encourage other people to be
affectionate and kind in return. Try to keep strong emotions
out of the equation and listen to what those closest to you
need. It's a good time to think about a holiday or a trip away
with a loved one.

Thursday 5th

Notice your stress levels at work after the festive break and consider where in life you can change your approach to take the pressure off. Look at where your priorities lie and how you can shift the balance to better suit your situation moving forward. Embrace technology and future ideas.

Friday 6th

Today's full moon highlights everyday matters, such as what you do for a living and how you spend your time. You may soon have some key decisions to make regarding your work, routine and lifestyle. Slow down the pace so you can contemplate what comes next.

Saturday 7th

If you're craving change, it's an excellent weekend to apply for a new job or rewrite your CV. If you want to get to know a work colleague better, consider arranging to meet up for a chat. Take the time to check in on your health.

Sunday 8th

Sunday is traditionally a day of rest, but your work, lifestyle and health are under the cosmic spotlight now. It's a great time to plan ahead, so line up some new and exciting goals. If you're looking for a way to create more freedom in your life, start as you mean to go on.

Monday 9th

Notice where in your life you're feeling rebellious. If you're a typical Leo, you like to be the boss and you don't always find it easy when other people tell you what to do. If you find yourself feeling like this today, try not to overreact.

Tuesday 10th

If you have a larger-than-life personality, you may find that it can sometimes seem threatening to other people. If you've been experiencing an ongoing issue with a colleague or partner, it could be amplified today. Do your best to ignore the issue and get on with the job at hand.

Wednesday 11th

The more positive you are at your place of work, the easier you will make life for yourself. Today is a great day to look at new ways of working and enjoy spontaneous conversations with your colleagues. List all the things you like about your job.

Thursday 12th

Mars's change of direction today indicates that friends and group activities are where the action's at. You're wise to be proactive in these key areas of life, so sort out any disagreements and get back on track. You may reconnect with someone you haven't heard from since October.

Friday 13th

Money could be a key factor in a work decision. It's a good time to help other people, but it's important to put yourself first sometimes to ensure both your good health and an emotionally fulfilling work routine. This evening, line up a social occasion with friends.

Saturday 14th

Love peaks this weekend, so a close relationship should provide the solace and sustenance you're looking for. It's important to have someone in your life who you can share your experiences with, someone who knows how to listen and is willing to share a burden with you.

Sunday 15th

You might feel detached or cut off from one person in your life right now, or you may be the one to choose to create some distance between yourself and a third party. Be aware that someone close might behave unpredictably today.

Monday 16th

Your plans may change suddenly, and you might recognise a divide between your home life and your career path. Juggling the work/life balance is rarely easy, so try to discover where the major issue lies and make a change. Your other half may have their own problems to deal with today.

Tuesday 17th

If you're lacking support either at work or at home, it's important to consider what you can do to change the situation. The day will get better as it goes on, so you should be able to put any challenges behind you this evening.

Wednesday 18th

It's an ideal day to give something up, particularly a bad habit. Consider what you need to release in the long-term if you're going to achieve a personal or professional goal. Listen out for news and be ready for a turning point.

Thursday 19th

If life's taken a serious turn recently, you're probably feeling disillusioned. Your situation will change again but for now, try to stay on track with what you want to achieve. Completing a deadline or finishing a writing project will give you a solid sense of satisfaction.

Friday 20th

The Sun moves into your relationship zone today. This spells good news for love and may bring about the chance to resurrect a relationship. Partner up with others, look for expert advice and find people who can help you. Don't go it alone over the next few weeks.

Saturday 21st

Today's new moon may offer you an opportunity to turn over a new leaf, put the past behind you and start again. If you're looking for love, don't hold back. Now that Aquarius, the sign of modern technology, is in your relationship zone, it's a good time to consider joining an online dating site.

Sunday 22nd

The new moon will highlight any areas in your life where you want to wipe the slate clean and start over. You might be ready to commit to a relationship or to say yes to a new source of expert advice in your life.

Monday 23rd

Think about creating new rules and boundaries in your key partnerships today, as doing so will benefit you professionally and help you get on the same page as a close work colleague. In personal relationships, it's important to know exactly where you stand.

Tuesday 24th

If you have a friend who's a renowned salesperson, they could come knocking today. Be wary of a financial scheme that sounds too good to be true. The best way to earn more money now is probably through your job. Consider picking up some overtime or applying for a different role.

Wednesday 25th

Look out for a person of influence and get on the right side of people who can help you today. If you widen your social network, you might hear about an opportunity to travel or study. This should be an exciting time for love, especially if you're able to celebrate a partner's good fortune.

Thursday 26th

You may be planning a spring holiday or a trip away over the Easter weekend. If you're feeling inspired, today is great to explore these options further. It's a good idea to have something to look forward to.

. . . .

Friday 27th

A relationship may enter a new stage today, and you could find yourself taking a big leap forward. Love and partnership often go hand in hand. The focus remains on relationships, so look to find harmony with the people closest to you.

Saturday 28th

It may be the weekend, but your stars are centred on your career and vocation. You might be working overtime or looking for a new job opportunity. If you get carried away and forget what time it is, someone close may be upset.

Sunday 29th

Technology is your friend today, because you have Uranus, the planet of innovation and future trends, in your career zone. This is a good opportunity for exploration, so get on board with what's new.

Monday 30th

You could make swift progress today, especially if you were able to put in extra hours over the weekend. You might find exactly what you're looking for online or be a whizz in a brainstorming session. It's a great time to apply for a job, ask for a promotion or locate the person who can best help you.

Tuesday 31st

If there's a friend in your life you're constantly falling out with, things could flare up again today. Alternatively, you might have an opportunity to make any romantic feelings known. Think about getting involved with a fitness group or a charity.

FEBRUARY

. . . .

Wednesday 1st

If you have a friend who likes to lead you astray, they might be back on the scene today, so be careful. Look out for the person playing the sensible role, perhaps your partner. Think twice before you do something you may regret later.

Thursday 2nd

It's an ideal day to be somewhere comfortable and cosy, so let your focus turn inward rather than out into the world. Meditation could be a big help today, and one of your friends might be the reason you decide to embark on a new journey.

Friday 3rd

If you can take the day off work today, it might be a wise move to do so, especially if you're feeling tired or low in energy. It could help to have some time to yourself rather than getting dragged into other people's lives. Your preference is likely to be to chill out this evening.

Saturday 4th

It's a day full of surprises, so be ready for the unexpected, particularly as other people may behave unpredictably. You might take yourself off on an adventure, especially if you feel you need a break from the person you see most weekends.

Sunday 5th

Full moons are often celebratory, dramatic and emotional, so you should put your needs first and ensure you're the centre of attention at some stage during the weekend. The full moon in Leo is a wonderful opportunity to grab the limelight and bathe in its glory. Trust your intuition.

Monday 6th

You may have to take care of other people more than usual now, or you might find yourself coming second today and feel less confident as a result. This is par for the course when the Sun, which rules vitality and energy, is as far away from your star sign as possible.

Tuesday 7th

Pay close attention to your finances today and get on top of things. You might fall out with a good friend over money, especially if you're feeling emotional about your situation. Sit down, write a list and get things down on paper.

Wednesday 8th

If you're typical of your star sign, you're generous, big-hearted and you love to help other people out when you can. It might be best to focus on yourself right now, but you can still share your love with those that need it.

Thursday 9th

You might come up with some brilliant ideas for a money-making venture while you're involved in a completely different activity. Sometimes being spontaneous helps you to find your creative side. Consider catching up with a relative or sibling.

Friday 10th

Your mind is likely to be super focused and able to solve any puzzles, riddles and conundrums that come your way today. Don your detective hat at work and get to grips with an issue that's been bothering you since the end of last year.

Saturday 11th

Talk planet Mercury enters your relationship zone today, so you won't be short of people to talk to. Even a quick trip to the shops could drag on, especially if you stop to talk to everyone you meet. You may find it hard to get anything done on a day like today.

Sunday 12th

Try your hardest to forget about work and serious issues today, and instead focus wholeheartedly on your family or your home. You may be ready to broach a sensitive matter with someone close, or perhaps you miss hanging out with those who know you best.

Monday 13th

You're never guaranteed to get on with your partner's family. If there are issues between you, they could come to the fore today and be a cause for concern. As much as you might try to work things out in your head, it's not always possible to make sense of what's going on.

Tuesday 14th

The moon is in your romance zone, and this is good news on Valentine's Day, as it means that it's a great time to ask someone out on a date. If you want to let someone who lives abroad know that you're thinking about them, reach out. A singles event this evening could be great fun.

Wednesday 15th

Try to think about money as a flow of energy: once you're 'in flow', life becomes easier. Today's stars are charitable and compassionate, so you should consider how you want to help the people in your life. Be creative and use your time well.

Thursday 16th

You may be under pressure from someone close today, perhaps a boss or a third party. See your relationships for what they really are and decide who you want to be around and who you want to move away from.

Friday 17th

The best-case scenario right now is that you have someone fighting your corner, someone who's doing their best to support and help you. There's the potential for a lively vibe at work, so being sociable could help you cope with your job, however mundane it may be.

Saturday 18th

The Sun's move into Pisces today is about money and finances, so you may be feeling creative about making or saving money, or you could be experimenting with new ideas around attracting abundance or wealth. Don't put all your financial eggs in one basket.

Sunday 19th

It's good to be clear about what you can and can't afford, especially if you're keen to travel. If you're linked to another person financially, a lot may depend on how they're doing. It's a good day to have a conversation about love or money.

Monday 20th

Love planet Venus moves into your travel and study zone today. If you're looking for love, this is a great time to embark on a holiday romance or to meet someone new on a course or at an evening class. It's also a good day to make an important agreement that benefits you in the long-term.

Tuesday 21st

While you may often be happy to live in a fantasy world, that's not the best place to be today, as reality could come crashing in. A conversation with a loved one might quickly turn into an argument, especially if they reveal something you didn't know about. Steer clear of an angry friend.

Wednesday 22nd

If things took a negative turn yesterday, focus on the positive aspects of life today. This evening, aim to bring two people together who've not been getting on well recently. You may have to act as the mediator, but it's worth it if you want them both in your life.

Thursday 23rd

You'll be feeling pleased with yourself if you've helped to resolve a falling-out. There's a social vibe today, so introduce your friends to one another or meet up with your partner's friends. Try to be around people who've got a lot to talk about.

Friday 24th

Getting to work may take you longer than usual. There could be problems on your commute, or with your mode of transport. Build some extra time into your work schedule, especially if you want to make a good impression at work. It's an excellent day to focus on your career and finances.

Saturday 25th

You may that you have to work at points over the weekend. This could be linked to your regular job or a new project that you're trying to get off the ground. If it's connected to an online business or shop, you're right to get excited about it.

Sunday 26th

You might have to ask your partner to be patient today, especially if you would rather focus on your career goals. They may not sound happy, but you need space to think about your success and future path. Create the time to catch up with your friends later on.

Monday 27th

Look to life outside of work today lining up some fun and games with your mates. You might enjoy talking about a holiday or group get-together that's coming up soon, or there could be some gossip doing the rounds about a friend's love life. Be at the heart of whatever's happening.

. . . .

Tuesday 28th

It'll be easy to get your wires crossed today, especially if you're involved in a complicated friendship. Mixing friendship and romance is rarely easy, and things may be trickier than usual now. Think about whether you want to have a serious talk later on to see where you stand.

MARCH
· · · · · · · · · · · · · · · · ·

Wednesday 1st
You may need more time to yourself today. Let your thoughts turn inward and begin to ponder the meaning of life. If a relationship is causing you some concern, take a step back and look at your emotions closely. It can be scary when you're on the verge of taking the next big step.

Thursday 2nd
Your partner's response to holiday plans could reveal more about what they're thinking. If they're excited that you're off somewhere exotic, that's great. However, if they're focusing on what might go wrong, it might take a heart-to-heart to get to the truth of the issue.

Friday 3rd
Today is a good day to chill out and take it easy. However, you may first have to deal with a sensitive issue that requires closer examination. Money matters are also under the cosmic spotlight, and are particularly relevant if you're keen to go on holiday now or in the future.

Saturday 4th
If you're looking for love, it's a great time to embark on a holiday romance or meet someone new at an evening class. Love has an exotic theme, whether you're dreaming of a lover abroad or craving more excitement in your current relationship.

Sunday 5th

The moon is in Leo all day today, and you should make the most of this by doing more of what you love. It's an excellent day to meet up with friends and talk about your next big adventure. You need stimulation now, especially if you're feeling bored by a mundane moment in life.

Monday 6th

The full moon cuts across the financial axis of your horoscope, and this means that it's likely to be an important week for money matters. Full moons often bring clarity, even if you're feeling emotional about what you value highly in life. Do what feels right and trust your intuition.

Tuesday 7th

Financial and emotional issues are often closely linked, and this is likely to be important now. You may feel a sense of sadness if you realise that you have to let go of something or someone; however, this could turn out to be a karmic experience. Think long-term and do whatever's necessary to feel safe and secure.

Wednesday 8th

A partnership or personal relationship may be entering a new phase and will demand more responsibility from one or both of you now. Think things through before making a long-term commitment. Turn to someone who's a good listener this evening, and they should respond to you honestly and fairly.

Thursday 9th

Throw yourself into life wholeheartedly today. The more positive you are about your next steps, the more confident you will become. It's a good day for studying or taking a test, so long as you read the instructions carefully. Too much bravado may cause you to come unstuck.

Friday 10th

You might peak too early today, whatever this means for you. Perhaps you're enjoying a boozy Friday lunch with friends or you're attacking an advanced fitness class with gusto. Whatever the case, it looks as if your energy could fizzle out later on. Pace yourself.

Saturday 11th

You might come up with some brilliant ideas today that could revolutionise your working life or your finances. If you're keen to get away with a loved one or you're organising a holiday, try not to let anything hold you back. Whatever problems arise, find a way to overcome them swiftly.

Sunday 12th

It's a lovely Sunday to share a special experience with your family and loved ones, especially if you're attending a celebration. Forget work for the day and instead concentrate on deepening your close relationships. Dare to talk about a sensitive or intimate issue.

Monday 13th

You may have a tricky conundrum to solve today, perhaps concerning a financial situation. You might not want to let a lack of cash stop you from doing something you love, but it's also important to make sure you don't jeopardise your future plans. Weigh things up and make the right decision.

Tuesday 14th

There may be an issue concerning love and relationships to deal with today. It's a good idea to go with the flow, so don't get embroiled in other people's dramas. Be there for others, but don't let their reputation impact your life.

Wednesday 15th

You might not be standing on solid ground today. Plans may be elusive and solutions could feel out of reach. Allow yourself to dream and conjure up new ideas. At the same time, ensure you're not looking at the situation through rose-tinted glasses.

Thursday 16th

Today is a good day to focus on teamwork and seek expert advice, so use your connections and your network. Finances will probably remain uncertain, especially if you haven't agreed on a contract or you're unsure of your position. Don't let this cause an argument. Be patient.

Friday 17th

Wherever there's uncertainty in your life, today could be an opportunity to start to move things forward in the right direction. A morning meeting or interview could bring the information or news you've been waiting for. Find the right expert to provide the help you need.

Saturday 18th

If you often find that being emotional doesn't help you, try to switch off your feelings and be more objective and rational about what's happening. Explore your current situation and try to solve a long-term issue.

Sunday 19th

Talk planet Mercury moves into your travel and study zone today, and this is a cue to bring more adventure into your life. If you're feeling swamped by personal or everyday issues, fire some metaphorical arrows high into the sky and see where they land. Line up a new experience or three.

Monday 20th

The Sun's move into Aries today should be a positive shift for you, because the Sun moves out of an emotional water sign into a motivating fire sign. If you've been coping with some disappointment recently, you should notice an energy shift and start to feel better about things.

Tuesday 21st

Today's new moon shoots you into the future, making this an ideal time to line up a new adventure. It's about expanding your horizons, exploring new cultures and saying yes to fresh experiences. If you're feeling bored or restricted in life, it's here where inspiration can be found.

Wednesday 22nd

It's a good time to look ahead, but don't put all your current plans on hold. Think long-term rather than short-term. The new moon phase highlights your horoscope zone and may help you to find meaning in life. Turn to philosophy and meditation to restore your spirits.

Thursday 23rd

If possible, try to take a breather from a long-term issue. If you sense you're getting nowhere with your current regime, do something radical and revolutionary instead. You might think about starting a business online, or you could encounter a new boss who's a force to be reckoned with.

Friday 24th

It could be a key moment for a long-term relationship or partnership. One of you could decide to follow your career path or vocation rather than investing in the relationship. Alternatively, a business might move online, triggering a redundancy for someone close.

Saturday 25th

Make time to process any recent big events that have changed your relationship. If necessary, take a step back and think about untangling yourself from an emotional connection. This may include a liaison that's about lust rather than love. Moving on starts with being kind to yourself.

Sunday 26th

Turn to a good friend for a chat today, especially if you're struggling to understand the behaviour of someone close to you. If you work with other people one-on-one, it might be wise to stop and consider whether you're over-giving and losing yourself in the process.

Monday 27th

It's an excellent day to plan your next big adventure with your best friend or a group of mates. If you're feeling tired or stressed, even more reason to line up some downtime or fun and games. Be around people who know how to lift your spirits.

Tuesday 28th

If you know you're stuck in a rut, this week's astrology provides the perfect opportunity to shake things up. Any activity that helps you to shift your perspective is recommended, whether you decide to go on retreat or you join in with a group of people who have new and innovative ideas.

Wednesday 29th

You can press the reset button for love today, especially if you work with someone you're close to. Today's stars may spell good news for your career and vocation, and you might hear about a new position or a recent hiring. If you can get the right people on your side, you will go far.

Thursday 30th

If you want to do something wild and entrepreneurial, go for it. While it's important to take good care of yourself and to think about other people in your life, you should also consider making space to try something new. Surf the wave of excitement that's crashing in.

Friday 31st

The moon is in your star sign, so this is your chance to take centre stage and strut your stuff. If you're a typical Leo, you know how to put on a show and you're very good at faking it until you make it. Go all out to make a good impression.

APRIL
. . . .

Saturday 1st

You may have some technology issues today. If so, this is a
sign that you need to switch off the computer and walk away
from whatever's not working. You'll enjoy yourself more if you
explore somewhere fresh and exciting. Be around new people
and broaden your horizons.

Sunday 2nd

If you're not great at budgeting or saving your money, you
might receive a wake-up call today. It's not always easy to
say no to an event when you can't afford it, but it's wise to be
realistic about cash. Rather than feeling down, try to use any
time to yourself constructively.

Monday 3rd

Talk planet Mercury moves into your career zone today, so
new opportunities may open up for you. If you're looking for
a job or you want to set up a meeting or interview, it's best to
act fast. If you're fed up with office politics, you might want to
shift your focus onto what comes next.

Tuesday 4th

Keep close tabs on your finances today and double-check
everything that's going in and out of your bank account. A lack
of concentration could cost you dearly, so try to remain alert.
A late-night conversation could be just the thing to leave you
feeling emotionally fulfilled.

Wednesday 5th

Look out for the right work partnership and talk about your career and vocational dreams today. If there's a chance to seal a deal, be persistent and try to make it happen. Be aware that it's best to complete any important matters before April 20th.

Thursday 6th

Today's full moon is about education, gaining knowledge and finding meaning in the world. Seek inspiration, learn something new and try to inspire others. Use the full moon to bring clarity to your current situation and make a decision about your next steps.

Friday 7th

If you allow yourself to dream during the full moon period, you may come up with a creative solution about how best to serve other people. Use your connections and reach out to people who can help you. It's an ideal day for mind-mapping and tapping into your guiding intuition.

Saturday 8th

Something related to your work might mean that you need to visit a hospital or prison today. Supporting other people will bring you great fulfilment, so do your bit to help. You could even ask your family to join in to support a good cause.

Sunday 9th

Make time for a member of your family today, especially if they need some advice about their next steps. You may be able to help them handle a person in a position of influence. Helping those around you suits your current astrology perfectly.

Monday 10th

It's the last day of the long weekend and your best chance to go off and have some fun. When you do more of what you love in life, your mood is likely to shift, so aim to spend more time with the people closest to you. It's also a good day to work on a hobby, skill or talent.

Tuesday 11th

It's a wonderful time to think about booking a holiday to give yourself something to look forward to. If you're keen to study and expand your learning, look out for new opportunities and trust your luck. It's a week for thinking big as the wheel of fortune turns in your favour.

Wednesday 12th

It might be a slow start to the day, especially if you feel unusually moody. Throw yourself into work or fitness and you'll soon be back on track. There's the potential for excitement at work, so listen out for the latest gossip. Friendship has the potential to turn into love now.

Thursday 13th

If you're setting off on holiday soon or you're back from a trip away, this will probably be the focus of your attention. It could be a challenge to concentrate at work or while completing your chores. An intense relationship may bring excitement, but make sure you stay safe if you're taking a big step.

Friday 14th

You may experience some disappointment today regarding either love or money. If you're around someone who lowers the mood, this could cause you to suffer a dip in energy. When it comes to a love or a relationship decision, it might be best to trust your head over your heart.

Saturday 15th

A quick way to improve a relationship is to go on a day trip or do something fun and adventurous together. Actions often speak louder than words, so throw yourself into life wholeheartedly and with gusto.

Sunday 16th

If you're back at square one regarding a close relationship, it might be a good idea to create some space between you, even if only for a short while. It might help to have some time to figure out what your emotions are telling you. Spending time alone could be exactly what you need now.

Monday 17th

It's likely to be a sensitive start to the working week, so it may not be possible to stop your emotions from flooding out today. You might want more intimacy with another person, but be wary of merging so completely that you lose yourself in the process. Some meditation time will help.

Tuesday 18th

If you had a good night's sleep, you should be ready to hit the ground running and get on with things today. So long as you have some fun built into your schedule, it's a great day to get motivated and fired up about the things you love. You might feel worn out later, but that's okay.

Wednesday 19th

What you learn via a course, workshop, book or conversation could pique your curiosity and set you on a new path today. New knowledge can prove to be inspirational and may spur you on to take the next step in your career.

Thursday 20th

Your ruler the Sun is involved in today's new moon before it reaches the pinnacle of your horoscope, and this is a sign that you may be ready for new beginnings in your career or your future path. Set your intentions for the future and say them out loud to the universe.

Friday 21st

You may have to take a step backward before you can take a step forward. Your destiny is not always in your hands, and a lot may depend on the actions or decisions someone else makes. If you've had enough of power games or feel out of control, the bold move is to retreat.

Saturday 22nd

If you have neither the answers you need nor a clear sense of direction, it might take you a few weeks to find a solution to a work-related problem or issue. You may explore lots of different ideas but find that nothing sticks, and this is to be expected when Mercury is retrograde.

Sunday 23rd

Call your friends and think about making plans to have fun. If it's been a big week for you on the work front, even more reason to switch off and have some frivolous fun. A flirtation or romantic encounter might be the icing on the cake.

Monday 24th

When it comes to your career plans and next steps, keep your thoughts to yourself for now. If you discover that someone isn't on your side, read between the lines and keep your cards close to your chest. An evening at home may suit you perfectly.

Tuesday 25th

Firm things up today to ensure you know where you stand, especially regarding your career. A partner, either personal or professional, may be caught up in everything that's happening, and might be the one initiating the big changes that are making things difficult at work.

Wednesday 26th

The rumour mill might be whirling madly today, but don't believe everything you hear, as it's a time of misunderstandings and untruths. In a similar vein, don't be tempted to overplay your strengths or promise more than you can deliver, and instead be realistic and discerning.

Thursday 27th

There may be someone in your life who you miss a lot right now. If grief and loss have been present in you for some time, be kind to yourself and put your needs first. Try to offload some of your responsibilities and consider taking an easier role at work if possible.

Friday 28th

If you've been experiencing some difficulties at work, these are likely to be especially pronounced today. Try to postpone a meeting or interview, especially if you know you're not ready or you're unsure of what you want to say. Give yourself up to love this evening or lean on a friend.

Saturday 29th

You may discover a unique way of solving an ongoing work problem today. Think outside of the box and get some input from your family or the people who know you best. Try to find new ways to take the pressure off.

Sunday 30th

Keep the conversation going today, especially if you want to come up with new ideas and solutions. Some things may not be entirely up to you, especially if other people are involved in making the decisions, so be sure to talk with everyone included in the process.

MAY

. . . .

Monday 1st

Something extraordinary may happen today, perhaps involving a boss or someone in a position of power. This might open a door for you to walk through. Let today's events could light the way for you to move into a new role.

Tuesday 2nd

There may be a lot to talk about if news of recent events filters through. Discuss all your options and keep the lines of communication open. This is an excellent time for fact-finding, research and gathering as much key information as possible.

Wednesday 3rd

If you're feeling out of sorts today, aim to keep your cool when expressing yourself. You might need to let off steam later on, either at the gym or by having a rant to someone who knows you well. Some big turning points are coming later this month.

Thursday 4th

If you need it, your friendship zone can offer an escape route, so gather good people around you. This is where you can find an outlet for your hopes and dreams. Turn to your groups to find activities that inspire you and touch your soul.

Friday 5th

Today's full moon links your past with your future. It's a powerful time to better understand what's made you who you are and who you're striving to become. Look back over the last two years and witness the big challenges you've overcome both at work and at home.

Saturday 6th

If you're looking for a new job or otherwise considering your future path, this month's full moon might open doors for you. Communication will be key to your success, whether you're sending off applications or making the most of your network. Think about ways to work smarter, not harder.

Sunday 7th

Self-love is one of the key themes in your current astrology. If you've been giving yourself a hard time recently, you may have the chance to change that today. Loving Venus moves into caring and kind Cancer, and this should open up an opportunity for you to be kind to yourself, so try to put your needs first.

Monday 8th

As you feel your way into the new week, it might be best to put off any major moves until later. Your stars light up the fun zone in your horoscope, so you may be in the mood to play rather than work hard. Plan something social for this evening and enjoy yourself, even though it's a Monday night.

Tuesday 9th

In what ways are you taking the lead in your career? What skills or talents do you have that are new and unique? What are you doing to be progressive and forward-thinking? These are the questions to ask yourself. Invite the unexpected into your life as a new path opens up for you.

Wednesday 10th

There may be a lot going on behind the scenes right now. Be aware that not everyone has your back: one person could be actively scheming against you. Dig deep to find out what's going on, but don't reveal more than you have to.

Thursday 11th

You may be itching to have a conversation with someone in your life right now, especially if you want to get to the bottom of something that doesn't make sense. Turn to someone close for their advice. You might get your chance to speak up next week, so be ready.

Friday 12th

What you want and what you need in life are not necessarily the same thing. Trying to walk your path sometimes means that you end up in opposition to people you care about. Take a step back if you can and try to view your situation objectively.

Saturday 13th

Do whatever's necessary to renew your passion this weekend. It's a good time to get back on a firm footing with your partner or someone else who's dear to your heart. If you want commitment, now might be the time to ask for it.

Sunday 14th

When money and emotions are closely linked, things can feel disorientating, and you are more likely to be led astray or influenced by others. It can be tough to balance spending with the need to keep your money safe and secure, so be discerning.

Monday 15th

As talk planet Mercury turns direct in your career zone, listen out for news about work and the things that you want to get out of life. Be wary of venturing into areas of life that unsettle you or make you feel uncomfortable.

Tuesday 16th

Jupiter, the planet of opportunity, moves into your career zone today, so notice any new opportunities that come your way. This could be the start of something big, and things that begin under Jupiter's influence often turn out well. Aim high and think big.

Wednesday 17th

You might feel a call to break free from something that isn't for you, perhaps because it doesn't allow you the space you need to pursue other goals. Consider your long-term aims and gear up to work hard over the next twelve months.

Thursday 18th

Allow yourself space to dream big as you visualise your next steps. This could turn out to be an exciting period for your career. If you're not on the right path, reorient your compass. If you know where you can make a difference, go for it.

Friday 19th

Today's new moon in your career zone favours the new, so get ready to embrace a new chapter. Consider what you need to let go of and what needs to change so that you can start afresh. Think about a new role or direction in life.

Saturday 20th

Your star sign is being powered up as action planet Mars enters your Leo, and this should boost your vitality levels and provide a cosmic confidence rush. Here's your chance to put yourself first: look after yourself before worrying about everyone else. It's your gig, so play it your way.

Sunday 21st

Your stars point to the theme of endings and letting go, especially regarding close relationships. This isn't a good time to go back to an ex. However, if you're ready to let go of a relationship that's toxic or based on control, your stars could prove to be a helpful influence.

Monday 22nd

Focus on your personal goals as well as your image and profile. People power is on the rise, and your stars favour joining in, showing your support and teaming up with others. You're bigger and better together, so feel proud of what you achieve.

Tuesday 23rd

If you've recently experienced a run of good fortune, you'll be on a confidence high. It's always gratifying when other people appreciate what you do and recognise your talents. Don't forget the value of being modest and humble.

Wednesday 24th

It may be a quiet start to the day, but that could change dramatically later on. Your zodiac symbol is the lion, and it seems there's a lot to roar about today. Take no prisoners and stride through life with confidence.

Thursday 25th

Don't waste your energy on a battle that's not worth fighting. When you step up in the world, you sometimes run into people who want to bring you down. If you're currently up against a tough opponent, it may be best to turn your back and concentrate on yourself.

Friday 26th

Look to the person in your life who loves you unconditionally and ensure you have their full support. When it comes to your work and career, this isn't a time to stick to tried and tested ideas. Ring the changes to keep your working life fresh.

Saturday 27th

You may be able to repay a loan or debt today, especially if you're doing well financially. Cutting ties will lift a weight and make you feel better. Your financial independence is likely to be important to you, especially if it was hard-won.

Sunday 28th

You may be up against some tough criticism today. Try to get to the root of the problem: if someone feels unhappy, they shouldn't take their mood out on you. It's best not to take an attack personally and to instead look at your situation truthfully. Take stock of where you are, what you're doing and where you're heading.

Monday 29th

If a financial situation is causing you some anxiety, try to relax and make the most of the long Bank Holiday weekend. A social vibe should kick in this afternoon, so you'll probably enjoy being around people who don't want to talk about work or the serious side of life.

Tuesday 30th

Be ready for a chance to restore balance and harmony in your life. Keep your conversations calm and on an equal footing. Choose your words carefully and let go of any recent upsets.

Wednesday 31st

You may be surprised if you hear news about a friend's love affair or secret romance today. If they reach out for support, be there for them and aim to be fair and considerate. If you're the one harbouring unrequited feelings, you might be able to open up soon.

JUNE

. . . .

Thursday 1st

If you're pulled in different directions today, you may begin to feel frustrated. A domestic crisis might require your full attention, whether you're negotiating with tradespeople or trying to sort out a family argument. Don't take on too much, and instead keep your expectations realistic.

Friday 2nd

Your situation is unlikely to remain steady today, especially if you're fed up with office politics or other people squabbling around you. Events at home might threaten to disrupt your career plans. Keep your gaze firmly on your future goals and put blinkers on if necessary.

Saturday 3rd

This weekend's full moon might indicate a big event for someone close to you or a personal change that needs to be addressed. You may choose to step in and help someone in your life, or you might be asked to arrange a major event or get-together. Do your bit for others.

Sunday 4th

Even though it's the weekend, the focus is on making changes. You might be learning about technological developments, especially as this is a sound period to keep up to date with new skills and qualifications. Immerse yourself in a study project and try to pass on what you learn.

Monday 5th

Lovely Venus moves into your star sign today where it will remain until mid-October. Make time for loving connections in your life, especially if it's been all work and no play recently. One relationship or business partnership could be under threat, so proceed cautiously.

Tuesday 6th

Seek new opportunities to shine bright, look your best and enjoy yourself. If a relationship has hit a peak of intensity, throw yourself into your work and escape by keeping busy. It's an excellent day for an interview or job application.

Wednesday 7th

It might be impossible to avoid dealing with a personal relationship today, especially if you're involved in a power game or a bid for control. Be wary of other people's motivations. Someone could turn nasty.

Thursday 8th

Be wary if someone is trying to make out that you're in the wrong. As you're a powerful fire sign, you sometimes end up in competitive situations. Ask yourself whether your pride is getting in the way of your progress.

Friday 9th

If you're concerned about an emotional issue, find someone to talk to who's caring and compassionate. This could be a therapist, a family member or your best friend. Make sure that your finances are secure by putting solid agreements in place.

Saturday 10th

Don't lose sight of your future goals, especially when it comes to finances. You may have to choose between money and love, or you could realise that you need to move away from a relationship or partnership. Even if it costs you, sometimes it's worth cutting the ties that bind you.

Sunday 11th

Look closely at a situation that's causing you a lot of stress. If in doubt, talk things through with a friend who knows you well. Being around other people will not only provide support, but fun too. It might be time to get back on the social scene.

Monday 12th

Take charge of your life by lining up an adventure. You may choose to be spontaneous and think about a holiday or trip away. If you've become embroiled in a tricky situation at work or in your personal life, even more reason to take hold of the reins and act decisively.

Tuesday 13th

Plans you make with friends during this time will be super exciting. You might be attending a new group or organising a big social get-together. Your career can bring you great fulfilment, but you're wise to focus on other areas of life too.

Wednesday 14th

You know you're on the right track when you're in flow and the wheel of fortune turns effortlessly. Even if what you're doing at work takes you out of your comfort zone, trust that life is moving you in the right direction. You may not be able to have it all right now, but you can enjoy what you do have.

Thursday 15th

You're one of the fixed star signs, which means you don't always respond well to change. When it comes to your work and career, you've probably had to alter things more than once recently. Stay focused on future trends. A friend could let you down, but this might save you money.

Friday 16th

Keep a close eye on money matters and make time to assess how to pay the bills or deal with debt. You might need to have a tough conversation with either yourself or a good friend. Take a step back and reconsider your options moving forward.

Saturday 17th

Your partner planet Saturn turns retrograde today, so you may choose to move away from a challenging relationship that's become a battle, or perhaps there's a significant shift or turning point that's out of your control. Don't rush into anything. Take your time.

Sunday 18th

Today's new moon takes place in your friendship and group zone, so it's a good weekend to reorganise your social life and line up something fun. If you're a typical Leo, you enjoy bringing people together and benefit greatly from group events. Be more sociable at work.

Monday 19th

Make an effort to shift things around and look to offload some of your responsibilities this week, especially if you've been holding on to too much recently. You may often gravitate to a position of leadership, but the stars are encouraging you to get more support on your side.

Tuesday 20th

It might be time to move further away from a friend who's let you down recently. You may find that you attract people who try to use you and feed off your generous nature, but it's better to have people in your life who you can trust.

Wednesday 21st

The Sun moves into Cancer, the star sign that rules retreat and inner work for you. This isn't about being out in the world, and instead means that it's an ideal time to focus on your personal growth and development. Take a step back and slow down the pace of life.

Thursday 22nd

Even though there might be a part of you that wants to hide away, you're still being called out into the world. One area of your life that may be buzzing with excitement today is your personal relationships. Aim to attract the one you want.

Friday 23rd

Get on top of money matters and remember to always read the small print. If necessary, close the door on the world so you can get to grips with a large amount of admin and correspondence. Whatever you're involved in, now is the time to focus on your security.

Saturday 24th

You might want to reassess where you can cut expenses and save money this weekend. If things are tight, ensure you're realistic and explore all your options. There may also be someone close to you who is struggling financially.

Sunday 25th

Be cautious around money and finances, even if your generous nature might mean that you want to help other people. Some financial schemes promise a lot but deliver little. Try to be savvy around money and help other people to do the same.

Monday 26th

Today's challenging astrology could flag up a personal issue or a confrontation at work. You may not be happy in your current job and find it a challenge to get on with your colleagues, employees or boss. The best advice is not to act impulsively but to instead wait for any heated situations to calm down.

Tuesday 27th

If you can create more quiet time in your life over the next three weeks, this would be a good idea, even if you have a busy work schedule. Remember that the bills still need to be paid. Take a moment to think about your place in life where you can help others.

Wednesday 28th

This is not the time to wing it, so you may have to get serious about your responsibilities. If you're helping someone close, you might have to make a tough call. If you have dependants, consider their long-term future as well as your own.

Thursday 29th

You may find that you're discussing money matters with people at home today. It's a good time to get your life in order, so try to create strong foundations for yourself and the ones you love. Protect your future.

Friday 30th

You might not like what you're having to deal with at the moment, but the stars indicate that it's important to do the right thing today. Take responsibility for your actions, as it could be a significant time for a big decision or step forward.

JULY

. . . .

Saturday 1st

Make the most of some beneficial self-care time by booking a massage or beauty treatment if this is what feels right for you. You should have some luck on your side today, so dare to dream big and line up some new goals.

Sunday 2nd

Today is a good day to trust yourself. Don't listen to other people if their ideas about what's right for you contradict your own opinions. Love will be lively today and could bring the unexpected your way. Try not to let another person's agenda knock you off course. Factor in some quiet time.

Monday 3rd

Today's full moon means that it's an ideal time to retreat and relax. Take a break from work if you can and pause to rethink your next steps. Keeping fit and healthy will help you deal with any changes to your routine. You're often happiest when you have a good work/life balance.

Tuesday 4th

You might be off work today, perhaps because you're feeling under the weather. You may need to slow down the pace of life, especially if you're being weighed down by a workload that's proving stressful. Learn from recent events and prioritise your wellbeing where possible.

Wednesday 5th

Look out for other people with whom you can collaborate today. You might need to show someone the ropes at work or have the chance to tell a third party about your current job and career goals. Reach out to other people and open your heart.

Thursday 6th

If you're currently in a relationship, be prepared for a reboot today. Try not to hold past behaviours against someone and focus on your future together instead. This doesn't mean that you should forget what's happened entirely, but practising forgiveness will help you as you move forward.

Friday 7th

You're unlikely to be the sort of person that lacks confidence, but today you might be feeling unusually shy. This could be because someone in your circle who brings out your vulnerable side, or perhaps you're around a person who challenges you intellectually. Deal with fear head-on and don't put yourself down.

Saturday 8th

Reconnect with your hopes and dreams for the future. You may not be able to give up the day job just yet, or perhaps your aim is to find work and improve your finances. In whatever way makes sense to you, restore your sense of hope.

Sunday 9th

If you're dealing with a personal issue, be kind and gentle with yourself today. A change of scenery might prove beneficial, so consider taking yourself off somewhere different. Take a closer look at your stress triggers and try to change a daily habit that doesn't benefit you.

Monday 10th

Money and work are calling you. Action planet Mars enters your money zone today, and this means that a quicker pace may be needed. It's a good time to pay close attention to your finances and to draw up a new accounting system or budget.

Tuesday 11th

Talk planet Mercury enters your star sign today, and this is your time to show off, find your voice and take centre stage. Life may speed up for you now, so be open to any invitation to make a presentation or talk to other people. Use your natural talents to help others.

Wednesday 12th

You may have to change your schedule to accommodate more distractions than usual today. Technology could either be your friend or your enemy. An online meeting might bring you into contact with someone who can boost your career in an unexpected way, so be ready.

Thursday 13th

It's hard to plan for the future if you're uncertain about your financial situation. Try to come up with some innovative ideas to strengthen your position. When it comes to your work and career, this is not the time to rest on your laurels or take your situation for granted.

Friday 14th

Stay on top of your career by lining up new plans and opportunities. The more future-oriented you are, the more successful you will be. Working from home will enable you to speed through your to do list.

Saturday 15th

Venus rules beauty as well as love and highlights your image and profile. This is an ideal weekend for a beauty treatment, haircut or any kind of personal makeover, especially if you're having photos taken for a website. It's best to do this before Venus turns retrograde in one week.

Sunday 16th

Even if you spend the whole day sleeping, you're still in tune with your stars. Today has the potential to be a serious chill-out day, so you might find that the less you do, the better. Doing nothing could help you to come up with your best ideas.

Monday 17th

Today's new moon points to the theme of endings as well as beginnings. It's a good time to consider what you're ready to let go of and where in life you want to release what's no longer working for you. Use the coming week to declutter, detox and prepare yourself for a new stage.

Tuesday 18th

The moon is back in your star sign today, so put your best foot forward and get on track with what you're planning. Your sign likes to shine from centre stage, so find the place where you can be the focus of everyone's attention. Perform at your best.

Wednesday 19th

If you're a typical Leo, you're likely to possess great conversation skills, and you should be able to talk yourself into anything today. Consider lining up an important meeting or scheduling a business lunch to impress someone in a position of influence. Alternatively, you might enjoy hanging out with your mates and having a gossip.

Thursday 20th

Try not to get into an argument over money today. If you experience a financial disappointment, do what you can to pick yourself up. You may not get the best financial advice today, so be careful about who you're dealing with.

Friday 21st

Try not to undervalue yourself or let someone else undervalue you today, as you're likely to feel more sensitive than usual right now. You won't appreciate harsh criticism, so keep thinking positively and focus on what you can do to better yourself and your position.

Saturday 22nd

You may have an insight about where you need to let go or bring something in your life to completion this weekend, perhaps concerning your work, lifestyle or fitness. Wherever you're carrying too much stress or pressure, take a step back.

Sunday 23rd

The Sun's move into Leo should boost your vitality and energy today, so you may want to be more proactive and take the lead in new events, or you might feel more sociable and be ready to let people see the real you. A love relationship, however, might take a backward step.

Monday 24th

Notice where in life you can take centre stage and do more so more often. This is a significant time to discover your creative skills and talents. Ensure that your current work/life balance allows you plenty of time to do what you love.

Tuesday 25th

If you're in a relationship, there may be a significant shift over the next few weeks. If there's a change in the level of support that one of you feels, now's the time to up your game. Use today's friendly stars to have an equal conversation.

Wednesday 26th

It's a good day to come together as a family to resolve a challenging situation. This may be related to one person in the family, or perhaps it's a joint issue that requires your attention. Focus on problem-solving and try to keep emotions out of the equation.

Thursday 27th

Love planet Venus is retrograde in your star sign, so this will be a deep and meaningful time in which you may undergo a stage of inner transformation. You may encounter temptation and hidden desires, but it's also a good moment to learn more about your passions that drive you.

Friday 28th

Talk planet Mercury enters your money zone today. For the next few weeks, you're wise to focus less on your personal life and more on your business and finances. If you're coming back from some time out, you might realise that you need to crack on with everyday matters.

Saturday 29th

When Venus is retrograde, it's generally not the best time to make a big change in your life. However, there are some days when the planet of love and beauty is well placed, and that's the case today. If you're single, someone from your past could come back into your life unexpectedly.

Sunday 30th

You might be working or busy around the house with domestic chores today. The more organised you are, the better. It's a good time to take good care of yourself by focusing on your health and fitness. Make a positive change in your routine.

Monday 31st

The productive vibe continues into the working week. When key planets are in earth signs, it's a good idea to turn your attention towards work and business. Put your emotions to one side, leave any personal dilemmas for another day and concentrate on the job at hand.

AUGUST

. . . .

Tuesday 1st

Today's full moon lights up both your identity zone and your relationship zone. Traditionally, full moons are a time of celebration, so think about doing something special with the one you love. If you're single and looking for love, use the full moon energy to draw up a wish list for your ideal partner.

Wednesday 2nd

Rather than allowing money worries to get on top of you, focus instead on what you're able to achieve at work and look for new opportunities to show other people how enthusiastic you are. Finding the right role model in your life can help to inspire you to reach new heights.

Thursday 3rd

Fear is a challenging emotion and, at its worst, can make you feel paralysed. What will help now is to write things down as an expression of what's worrying you. Voice your concerns and activate your problem-solving nature.

Friday 4th

Your psychic sensibilities may be strong right now, so tune into your feelings and lose yourself in the realm of your imagination. Your emotions can be a powerful creative source, so tap into the universal flow, as doing so should help you to realise that all will be well.

Saturday 5th

The moon is in your travel and study zone, and encourages you to broaden your horizons and make the most of life. The Sun is in Leo, so it's the perfect time for you to think about a holiday or trip away. Step out of your comfort zone and embrace a new adventure.

Sunday 6th

There's an easy flow to your stars this weekend, so make the most of this by doing more of what you love and showing off your natural abilities, skills and talents. You might discover the interests and passions that activate the depths of your soul.

Monday 7th

The feel-good vibe continues into the working week. If you're going to be successful, you may need to show off your true personality and unique skills. If you're typical of your star sign, you're likely to have an extroverted nature, and this can help you make a big impact on a person of influence.

Tuesday 8th

The more energy and enthusiasm you show at work, the more likely you are to be noticed. You might be involved in an audition or be interviewing for a new role or position. Wherever you're making your mark, take centre stage.

Wednesday 9th

You might discover something about a past relationship that comes as a shock today. Someone may accidentally reveal a truth about a partner that you were oblivious to. If this doesn't impact your life anymore, let it go. Otherwise, you may have some deep thinking to do.

Thursday 10th

If you're on a roll at work, make the most of this moment. You currently have some lucky stars, so you might hear good news today. If you're looking for work, it's an excellent day to apply for a job, while if you're involved in employing someone new, you might find the perfect candidate.

Friday 11th

If you have a friend who's a bad influence, they may be back with a vengeance today. This is all well and good if you only engage in innocent shenanigans, but make sure that you remain safe and secure.

Saturday 12th

Catch up with chores or sleep today, whichever you prefer. If you're recovering from a busy week, pencil in some relaxation time. If you've been neglecting your home, it's a good moment to try to bring a sense of order and calm to your home.

Sunday 13th

Love planet Venus remains retrograde in your star sign, so your relationships may be going through a strange phase right now. Follow your instincts and do what feels right. Today's stars could help you to charm your way into a person's heart.

Monday 14th

The Sun remains in your star sign this week, so it's an ideal time to put yourself first and do more of the things you love. Ensure you're enjoying work and play equally as you line up some new goals and intentions for the year ahead.

Tuesday 15th

Consider how best to put yourself first and shine bright in life. This is the moment to find new ways to promote yourself, especially online. If you want to be on top of your game, think about getting help from someone that can lift you up and take you to the next level.

Wednesday 16th

The best news this week is that today's new moon in your star sign. A new moon is a symbol of new beginnings, so this is the equivalent of your astrological New Year's Day. Make a wish when you first see the crescent moon in the night sky.

Thursday 17th

If you've been spending excessively recently, it's a good time to rein things in. What you don't want is to have your credit card declined or an overdue bill show up on your doorstep. Keep a close eye on money matters to prevent this from happening.

Friday 18th

It's a good day to get creative around money matters, whether you're looking to earn more or dealing with a debt situation. Use technology to keep up to date with everything that's happening and make sure you double-check everything.

Saturday 19th

You might choose to have a lie-in, especially if you were awake worrying last night. Take things slowly and spend the day close to home. It's a good time to be sociable, so you might try to find out what's going on in your local community or catch up with a sibling on the phone.

Sunday 20th

The social vibe continues today, so consider thoroughly exploring your local neighbourhood. You might come across a community event that piques your interest. It's also important to back up your computer and deal with any important correspondence before Mercury turns retrograde.

Monday 21st

You may not get a lot done at work today, especially if there's plenty of gossip doing the rounds. You might be enjoying the social vibe and catching up with your colleagues after a lively weekend. One way or another, it looks as if there's a lot to talk about. Put your feet up at home this evening.

Tuesday 22nd

Be clear about your motives around money matters. If you're worried about someone else's money management, consider sitting down and talking things through with them. A clear plan will be beneficial for everyone.

Wednesday 23rd

Turn your attention to finances and consider your possessions, what you own, your values and your self-worth. This is a great time to focus on your budget and your money mindset.

Thursday 24th

Mercury retrograde is the trickster, so it's important to be cautious around money over the next few weeks. An issue with your partner or an ex could cause some dissatisfaction. Alternatively, someone close to you may have a situation that requires your attention.

Friday 25th

Your stars look great for getting things done today, especially if you're wrapping up a project or dealing with finances. You're likely to have tremendous willpower and concentration right now. Focus on the finer details of life, but don't lose sight of the bigger picture.

Saturday 26th

There's some tough astrology looming this weekend, so you will need to face facts and be realistic about what's happening. If a relationship or partnership is holding you back, think about whether it's time to move on. If money's an issue, work out a plan for the future.

Sunday 27th

Action planet Mars enters Libra, the sign of balance, so aim to build harmonious relationships now. Listen to another person's point of view and, where necessary, work towards reconciliation. You don't want unnecessary conflict in your life, so make plans accordingly.

. . . .

Monday 28th

You might be unable to put off facing a relationship issue today. Work commitments may require your time and energy at the start of this week, but come this afternoon or evening, it might be necessary to reach out and agree to talk. You may not like everything you hear, but it's good to get the ball rolling.

Tuesday 29th

The best way to work with your stars today is to change things around, embrace freedom and find a way to renew your connection with your career and future path. This might mean that you have to be flexible, especially if life steps in and moves you in a new direction.

Wednesday 30th

If there's an ongoing issue within a long-term relationship, it might be best to broach the matter directly, rather than trying to avoid what's happening. Set a date and time when you can work things through.

Thursday 31st

There's a full moon today, so it may prove to be an emotional week, especially if you're experiencing strong feelings linked to money, such as guilt, envy and frustration. Know that you'll feel your emotions deeply at this time, and let them guide you.

SEPTEMBER

. . . .

Friday 1st
You may be looking for someone new to help you resolve an ongoing personal issue. If you need to negotiate with someone from your past, it might help to get a third party involved. Do what feels right for you.

Saturday 2nd
It's a great weekend to head off on holiday or go somewhere completely new. Changing your surroundings can help to shift your perspective on what's happening at home. Sometimes you can only view your situation objectively when you step away.

Sunday 3rd
Make a pact with someone close to avoid discussing work while you're off having fun; you can confront any important issues later on. For now, close the door on the serious stuff and put the fizz back into life.

Monday 4th
If you've had your eye on something special, today's stars could coincide with a gift or some good advice. Notice who you'd like to back you and think about where you can ask for support.

Tuesday 5th

Your career stars remain lucky, but you may need to take a step back to reassess your long-term goals, especially those linked to a love relationship or something else happening in your personal life. Now that Venus is direct, you should have a better idea about where you stand.

Wednesday 6th

Get the right people on your side and do what you can to secure your prospects. Be knowledgeable rather than scared about money. The more you know, the easier it is to make wise decisions. You might have a moment of inspiration.

Thursday 7th

Be cautious if you're thinking of asking a good friend to make you feel better. You might want them to agree with you, but they won't necessarily see your side of things. It may be wise to trust your own counsel rather than listening to what other people have to say today.

Friday 8th

Look out for any new opportunities or good news that comes your way today. Think about taking a risk and being more expansive. The more positive you are, the more in sync you will feel. This is the time to believe that good things are coming your way.

Saturday 9th

Try to stop holding on to any emotions or suspicions that are pulling you back. It's easy to fall into automatic behaviours, but today you should try to challenge any habits that aren't good for you. Break out of your routine.

Sunday 10th

Allow time for a good cry first thing if you know doing so will benefit you. It's an ideal day for an emotional release. Bump self-care high up your priority list and put your wishes first. Once the moon enters your star sign in the late afternoon, you're more likely to be ready to face the world.

Monday 11th

There are some serious feel-good vibes when it comes to love and relationships, so reach out to other people today. You might catch up with a sibling or relative at lunchtime and be with the one you love this evening, and this could lead to an experience that reminds you of the first time you got together.

Tuesday 12th

You may find that you don't want to toe the line or do what other people say today. There's a rebellious edge to your stars that you're wise to be aware of. Your big Leo character could make waves in the right arena, but don't upset your boss just because you're feeling edgy. Watch your step.

Wednesday 13th

When it comes to money matters, it might be best to avoid big moves where possible. There's a new moon on the way, so new beginnings are highlighted. This coincides with Mercury bringing the news or information you require.

Thursday 14th

You're right to hope that a change of fortune is coming your way. It's possible that you've not been aware of the full picture, or that someone has been keeping key information from you. It won't be long before you should have more information about where you stand.

Friday 15th

Today's new moon in your money zone coincides with Mercury turning direct after three weeks of being retrograde. Put the two together and there's a chance that there'll be good news for money matters, especially if your finances have been chaotic over the last couple of weeks.

Saturday 16th

Mercury's change in direction promises a positive shift, so aim to speak up about something important, even if it concerns an area of life that you prefer to avoid. Ask for what you want and make a determined effort to sort out a big issue.

Sunday 17th

The two best planets, Venus and Jupiter, come together today, and this links your personal life and future path. You're likely to be delighted about what's happening, especially if there's a change in your status, or good news for your partner that gives you both reason to celebrate.

Monday 18th

Work alongside your family today to ensure you have all the support you need. In a similar vein, it's a good time to reach out and make sure the people closest to you are doing okay. Having a strong support network can be a real boon and will help you to believe that anything's possible.

Tuesday 19th

This is an important time for you to think things through and focus on your inner wants and needs. Don't feel you have to rush into a major decision, and instead consider waiting to see what opportunities flow your way. Let go of any insecurities and realign yourself with your true value and self-worth.

Wednesday 20th

Life feels a lot easier when you have good people on your side and the mood at home is warm and caring. If someone is continually disruptive in your life, you may need to consider whether your relationship benefits you or them. Step up and tackle your responsibilities this evening.

Thursday 21st

You might be ready to transform the way you work, perhaps by choosing to be at home more or passing on some of your responsibilities to other people. Health is another factor to consider, especially if you want to ease stress levels for yourself or the people you care about the most.

Friday 22nd

An emotional issue may require you to prioritise someone else in your life, even if this means dropping what you're doing to be there for them. This might force you to work late or put in some extra hours of overtime.

Saturday 23rd

The Sun changes star sign today. This is a positive shift for you as it should mean a move away from finances and towards communication and connection. This is your chance to perfect your people skills, so try to make time for other people, both personally and professionally.

Sunday 24th

Notice who you enjoy being around and the difference between easy connections and people who drain your energy. It's better to veer towards the former and away from the latter, both at work and in everyday life. This could be the moment to take a step back from people or jobs that tire you out.

Monday 25th

Good news is a key theme in your life today. This might link back to what took place on August 10th or September 4th and could be about money or work. There may be an opportunity for you to succeed at something at the second or third time attempt. Consider what this means for you.

Tuesday 26th

You will need to use all your people skills to deal with a tense situation either at work or in your personal life today. Other people's behaviour could surprise or shock you and will require careful handling. You might need to consider whether you're the right person to step in.

Wednesday 27th

If you're keen to book a holiday or a trip away, get to grips with the financial aspects sooner rather than later. It's important to put a plan in place, and this is a good time to do so.

Thursday 28th

The light of the moon is at its brightest in the night sky now, and this should provide you with a sense of clarity. Tap into your intuition and decide whether the time is right to expand your horizons. Sometimes you have to follow a dream before you know how to deal with the practicalities.

Friday 29th

Today's full moon may coincide with a pivotal moment, and means that it's a good time for making decisions that involve both your head and your heart. It's a strong weekend for talking, meetings and get-togethers. Your love life is a different story, however, and an on-off relationship could be off again.

Saturday 30th

It's an ideal weekend to get away for a break or to do something that inspires you and changes your perspective. Try to find an innovative way to raise funds for a trip or course, perhaps involving a hobby.

OCTOBER

· · · · · · · · · · · · · · · · ·

Sunday 1st

If you're having a career rethink, there could be a significant turning point at the beginning of 2024. This is a great day to reconsider your long-term goals, where you're heading and why. Try not to let money become your main motivator, and instead look to rediscover your deeper purpose.

Monday 2nd

Venus, the planet of love and relating, remains in your star sign for one more week, and this is ideal for boosting your popularity and winning other people over. Feel your way into the coming week by doing more of what you love.

Tuesday 3rd

It's a good day to finalise an important decision, and doing so will help you feel more secure not only financially but emotionally as well. Try not to waste your precious energy comparing yourself to other people, and focus instead on what's possible for you.

Wednesday 4th

Be around other people and share your ideas with one another. The moon is in a social zone of your horoscope, encouraging you to use your networks and team up with other people. Let someone else step in and take the lead when it comes to organising a big event.

Thursday 5th

Talk planet Mercury enters your communication zone today, and this is a cosmic cue to talk, communicate and negotiate. If you're wary of someone's motives or behaviour, speak up. If you feel you need help or support, reach out. Consider your next study option.

Friday 6th

Balance your time equally between people and solitude. If you don't have enough space for yourself, you may soon begin to feel frustrated. Also, time alone is when you're at your most creative, so good ideas should spring to life.

Saturday 7th

Avoid anyone who's out to cause trouble today. It's not the best time to engage in bad behaviour or get involved in an argument. Fanning the flames of a fall out is often a bad idea, so it might be better to take a step back and agree to sort things out at a later date.

Sunday 8th

If you're in a relationship or married, have a conversation and try to get on the same page as each other. Wherever your life is out of balance, consider what needs to change. If you can work well together, you'll be a stronger unit.

Monday 9th

It's a strong week for talking, debating, meetings and get-togethers. However, you may need to be resilient, especially if there's pressure on you to get things right. You might need to prioritise work or other people, so it will be tricky to put yourself and your own needs first.

Tuesday 10th

If something's got to give, it may be time to decide that your job is more important than office politics, especially if you've had enough of feeling powerless. Whether you decide to embrace freedom or stick to your routine, it could feel like a no-win situation. Once you accept this, it's an easier choice to make.

Wednesday 11th

Don't take your foot off the pedal, especially if you're starting to make good progress with your plans. You have Jupiter, the planet of opportunity, in your career zone, so remain focused on your long-term goals. This period will last until May 2024, so factor this into your decision making.

Thursday 12th

There might be a significant turning point at home or within your family now. If you're waiting on an important deal, today's positive move may prove to be the equivalent of a green light. Doors will open for you, so it's a good time to chase up any matters relating to your home and family.

Friday 13th

Friday 13th often lends itself to superstition, but today's astrology suggests that no misfortune will occur, and that you may even have the chance to strengthen your position. Get backing from a family member and try to make moves that put you on a firmer footing in your personal life.

Saturday 14th

If you have a deep conversation with someone this weekend, you might find that your words have the power to create a soulmate connection. Any communication shared during this eclipse period could be life changing.

Sunday 15th

A new eclipse cycle is beginning, so it's a good time to consider your qualifications and your level of education. If you're lacking knowledge, this may become evident to you now, especially if you've failed an exam and need to rethink your next steps. Keep close tabs on a sibling.

Monday 16th

Your ruler the Sun is in air sign Libra this week, and this means that you should turn your attention to matters concerning communication. Libra is the sign of balance, but this week's astrology might feel more like walking a tightrope. It may be a challenge to keep talk light, especially if deep issues surface again.

Tuesday 17th

Dive into your past now and over the next few weeks by revisiting your childhood home or dealing with an issue attached to your parents. Doing so may bring up strong emotions, especially those linked to memory and feelings of loss.

Wednesday 18th

It's important to enjoy yourself and have some fun, so long as you don't blow your budget. If you have a friend with expensive tastes, it might be better to take charge of organising a social get-together yourself. It's always possible to find great ways to enjoy yourself on the cheap.

Thursday 19th

It's a good day to catch up with your relatives and those closest to you. Sharing experiences can sometimes be more rewarding than sharing gifts. This evening, talk to a family member about their interests and talents.

Friday 20th

If you're awake at dawn, you may have a moment of inspiration, especially if your mind is already fully alert. It's a good day to think about a new form of study, workshop or course. Commit to whatever helps you escape the mundane side of life.

Saturday 21st

You may need to have a tough conversation this weekend if something isn't working out. Decide where your limits lie, what you're capable of and when you need to take a step back and let go. Be wary of individuals who thrive on power and control.

Sunday 22nd

If a partner experiences a success today, this will be great news for both them and you. Talk through your next steps with your family and get everyone on board with what you're planning. If you're looking to make a big change, someone close may be able to support you.

Monday 23rd

The Sun's move into Scorpio should turn your attention towards home and family matters today. If you've not been spending enough time at home or been too busy to hang out with someone, here's your chance to readdress the balance. Prioritise family time or visit someone from your past.

Tuesday 24th

The stronger your team, the more secure you will feel. Try to build firm foundations at home or your place of work. It's a good day to set up a savings plan and to consider investing in your future. Deal with the serious side of life.

Wednesday 25th

If you're talking to someone in your family about finances and money management, technology may have an important role to play today. This is a good time to take lessons learnt from past mistakes into account.

Thursday 26th

Try to be more philosophical about what's happening and take a broader view of your current situation. You may feel trapped, but there are always options and ways to break free. Consider the bigger picture and find wisdom in history or literature.

Friday 27th

If you can take today off work to explore somewhere new, it might be a great idea to do so. Consider taking someone else's wisdom on board, especially if it comes from a trusted source. Try to get a broader perspective on recent events.

Saturday 28th

Today's lunar eclipse lights up the foundations of your horoscope. On the one hand, this is about your home, family and your connection to the past. On the other hand, it's about your career and your future path. Getting the balance right between these areas is the key.

Sunday 29th

There could be some furious arguments today, especially if there have been significant events in the previous two years. Big changes may have impacted your family or your career path. Aim to let go of any resentment or sadness and take responsibility for your part in anything that's happened.

Monday 30th

If events came to a head over the weekend, see what life is telling you and decide what steps you can take to move things in the right direction. You may decide that you're ready for more stability and less change in your life. Learn from recent events and try to move on.

Tuesday 31st

If there's a social occasion this Halloween, make sure you receive your invitation. Being around other people and having fun is the ideal antidote to any tensions that have dominated your life recently. Treat yourself and the ones you love.

NOVEMBER

. . . .

Wednesday 1st

Be wary of any unpleasant emotions today. You might be envious of a friend or feeling guilty for one reason or another, perhaps because of something that is linked to friendship or your close relationships. Try not to let your mood drop. This evening, take some time out and be kind to yourself.

Thursday 2nd

Take the pace slow, especially if you're dealing with a personal issue or your self-esteem has taken a knock. What's important today is that you do what's right for you, so put yourself first and appreciate the simple things in life. When you have a safe base, everything else will fall into place.

Friday 3rd

Wherever you've been feeling weak or unsure, you're likely to feel empowered today. Fact-finding could have an important part to play, because once you know where you stand, you can take action. Try to protect or even boost your reputation.

Saturday 4th

The wheels of change are turning, urging you to keep your gaze on the future without losing your connection to the past. One conversation might be challenging, especially if it involves a matter that's weighing on you heavily.

Sunday 5th

Be ready to deal with matters at home and within your family today. If you need to broach a difficult subject, step into your power before doing so. When you're brimming with self-confidence, you can tackle anything. Dig deep to find out what's going on beneath the surface.

Monday 6th

Start the week as you mean to go on by getting back on track with money and work goals. Don't let a home or family issue get in the way of what you want to achieve. When you find someone who can help you, doors start to open, so appeal to a person of influence.

Tuesday 7th

It's a good day to visualise your dream home or be caring and compassionate towards a family member. Even if they've behaved badly recently, try to reconnect with your love for them. An open conversation may be a big help.

Wednesday 8th

Venus, the planet of relating, moves into Libra and your communication zone today. This is a reminder that your relationships fare best when they're equal, fair and honest. If you've been giving too much recently, point this out to someone close. Step up your game.

Thursday 9th

Get back on good terms with the people in your life who are important to you. If last month's eclipses coincided with challenges, decide where you need to rebuild or recommit in your life. At the end of the day, blood relatives mean a lot, so consider your position within your family.

Friday 10th

Where do you feel you belong and where do you feel left out?
Some people may not appreciate you the way you want them
to, and this could cause an argument. If you're involved with
someone who's often unavailable, matters might come to a
head today. Be realistic about your situation.

Saturday 11th

Today's astrology suggests tension is likely around your work/
life balance, especially if you're finding it hard to divide your
time equally. Try not to be overly impulsive and don't let
tempers flare. It might be wise to take a step back, whether the
issue is at work or regarding your family.

Sunday 12th

Aim to deepen your close connections, especially with family,
relatives and the people in your life you've known for years.
You'll be acutely aware of what home and family mean to you
during this period of the year, so consider whether family may
need to come before your work.

Monday 13th

Today's new moon falls in your home and family zone, so it's
an ideal day to start over. Try to reconnect with family or think
about finding somewhere new to live. You may be faced with a
tough decision if your plans take an unexpected turn.

Tuesday 14th

Make time for someone close to you today, especially if recent
events have been unsettling for them. You may have to put
some new guidelines in place to protect their emotions. A
friend who lives locally could be a great source of advice.

Wednesday 15th

When you have friendships that are based on kindness and equality, this rubs off on the people around you. It's a good time for a social get-together with someone new, as doing so may prove beneficial for both of you.

Thursday 16th

Today's astrology is good for productivity and organisation, so get on top of work matters and sort out any outstanding correspondence at home. Pay close attention to the mind-body-spirit connection too; when you feel good about yourself, your energy improves and you automatically get more done.

Friday 17th

It's a good day for getting things sorted at home or within your family. It's here where you're wise to go in deep, whether you're helping someone close to you or talking about home renovations. Make sure that the people that matter to you know how much you care.

Saturday 18th

It's important to work alongside family members if you want to get more done today. You might be leap into a domestic project, whether someone's moving house or you're decorating together. Channel your passion constructively and release any pent-up tension. Be proactive and bold.

Sunday 19th

Make time for the one you love today. If life's taken over recently and you've not had enough time for one another, it's an ideal day to make amends. Keep things light and do something fun together later on.

Monday 20th

Other people could get in the way of your plans first thing today. It's never ideal to start the working week with an argument, but you may not be able to avoid a stand-off situation. If you need to stand your ground, do so. Don't give in to an ultimatum or unreasonable demand.

Tuesday 21st

If you're concerned about a big issue, it's a good day to consider your options. You may be able to appeal to someone's compassionate nature, so ask for more time to sort things out. Keep your emotions in check.

Wednesday 22nd

Your ruler the Sun enters Sagittarius today. This is good news for you, as Sagittarius highlights the good things in your life, such as romance, creativity, self-expression and hobbies. You should feel especially lucky now, so do something special and make the most of life.

Thursday 23rd

If there's something stopping you from leading the life you choose, this doesn't mean that you need to be unhappy about your current situation. Instead, appreciate all that you have in your life and find cheap ways to enjoy yourself. Be around people who raise your spirits.

Friday 24th

Fire sign energy kicks in this week, and this is good news for you, as it brings the feel-good factor to events. This energy is great for socialising, having fun with your family and enjoying good times. Someone close to you may finally open up for the first time in a while.

Saturday 25th

You may feel disappointed with someone close to you, or you might find that you need to step in and be there for someone you love who's currently struggling. Try not to get too caught up in any kind of argument or falling-out.

Sunday 26th

Focus on what's working well for you at the moment and strike while the iron's hot. This is an ideal weekend to arrange a date, enter a competition or hang out with your family. Be spontaneous and aim to put a smile on the face of someone you love today.

Monday 27th

Today's full moon cuts across the social axis of your horoscope. If you're invited out early this week, consider prioritising fun over work or other commitments. Be willing to let go completely and put any challenging issues to one side.

Tuesday 28th

Your stars feel indulgent and lazy today, so you might find it hard to be proactive or be unable to get things done. Instead, allow yourself to daydream and go with the flow. This energy might reveal something important about your relationship with someone close.

Wednesday 29th

If you're typical of your star sign, you love helping other people. Before you leap in, however, make sure you're doing so for the right reasons. If you find it hard to say no, be aware of this tendency. A slower pace will benefit you today.

Thursday 30th

If you're trying to break a bad habit, you need to be strict with yourself, especially when you're faced with temptation. Focus on the reasons you want to make the change and take your time rather than giving in. Being spontaneous at your place of work could pay off for you.

DECEMBER

Friday 1st
Pay attention to the conversations you have around work and health, as this area of your life may become more important now. Seeds that are planted this week could stir your dreams and get you fired up for new beginnings in the year ahead. If you keep repeating yourself, change the script.

Saturday 2nd
New habits don't get put in place without commitment. If you're serious about a fitness goal, do whatever it takes to stay on track, whether this means being accountable to a buddy or signing up for a gym membership.

Sunday 3rd
While you probably don't like unnecessary conflict in your life, there are times when an argument is unavoidable. You might need to have a tough conversation this weekend, especially if things aren't working out between you and someone close. Steer clear of individuals who thrive on power and control.

Monday 4th
Consider what you invest in and where you can make changes to boost your wellbeing. Think about seeking help from an expert who can help with an ongoing issue or complaint. If you're interested in interior design or otherwise making your home beautiful, you're in tune with your stars.

Tuesday 5th

You might be getting the house ready for the festive break, especially if you have family coming to visit. Today's stars feel productive, so you should be able to get a lot done. Be firm when it comes to family arrangements and ensure you're all on the same page.

Wednesday 6th

If you're worried about something, it's a good time to seek activities that whisk you away from the realities of life. Taking time out to dream and feel inspired can often be a good idea. Enjoy a day trip to the sea or a walk by a river. Do something indulgent and pamper yourself.

Thursday 7th

If work has been a slog or you've been unemployed for a while, the pressure should start to ease now. The more you focus on doing what you love, the happier and more fulfilled you will be. Make time for yourself.

Friday 8th

Your stars may provide answers to a work conundrum. If you're looking for a way to create more freedom in your life, focus on your ideas for next year. Do the same if you're looking for work. Expand your network and find something that fits what you want to do.

Saturday 9th

It's an ideal weekend to visit family or catch up with your relatives. This time of year is often poignant and is likely to remind you of the ones you love and where you come from. There may be an addition to the family, perhaps a birth or the arrival of a new pet.

Sunday 10th

If you're finding it hard to achieve a healthy work/life balance, find ways to use technology to free up your time. If you're super keen to get organised over the festive period, draw up a spreadsheet and share it with your family.

Monday 11th

If there's someone you've been meaning to talk to, it's a good day to reach out. Try and reconcile any family differences before the festive period. If someone close continues to need your support, be there for them and ensure they receive the right kind of advice.

Tuesday 12th

Today's new moon highlights the fun zone of your horoscope, which includes romance, creativity, entertainment, good fortune and luck. The more you put into your life, the more you get back in return.

Wednesday 13th

Talk planet Mercury turns retrograde today. This often indicates hold ups and delays, so things might not progress as you expect and work may prove to be unpredictable. You might have to come up with a new solution to an old problem, so be willing to rework and revise your plans.

Thursday 14th

Mercury is retrograde now, so it's a good time to try again where you failed once before. This might mean reapplying for a job or getting back in touch with someone from the past. You should have some luck on your side at the moment, so it might be worth asking for what you want.

Friday 15th

Do your best to complete your chores or meet a work deadline now so that you have the weekend free to enjoy yourself. Harness all your willpower and do whatever's necessary to concentrate on the job or task at hand. This evening, turn your attention to love and relationships.

Saturday 16th

If there's a lot to do at home, try not to get bogged down by the boring stuff. Today looks brilliant for romance and passion, so if there's someone you fancy but you haven't let them know, this could be the evening to do so.

Sunday 17th

You may feel disheartened about a financial matter or money in general, especially if you've been buying Christmas gifts that are beyond your budget. Remember that love and kindness are the best presents you can give anyone.

Monday 18th

Today may bring you a second chance at something you've been hoping to achieve. It's worth going the extra mile if the right opportunity arises. Alternatively, you might try to negotiate your way into a better position. It's worth setting things up now so you can start afresh in the new year.

Tuesday 19th

You may find that money matters are a cause of concern right now. If you simply need to change your attitude, work on your festive mindset and try to find creative solutions. If you have a giving nature, you might need to rein in your expectations for the moment.

Wednesday 20th

If you hear someone's plans have changed and you won't be meeting up now or over the festive period, try to be philosophical. It may not be anyone's fault, especially if one of you has a busy life. Try not to overreact and, if in doubt, be kind. You might find that you're up late tonight.

Thursday 21st

You're wise to be flexible today, as your stars suggest you may have technology problems or clash with someone over an important issue. Take a step back if necessary. If the issue involves family, make sure you sort things out as soon as possible. Try to put other people first.

Friday 22nd

A steady routine is ideal at this time of year. Look after yourself and be organised and efficient in getting things done. You might find that you're working over the festive season, especially if you want to do your bit to help others.

Saturday 23rd

Today's stars may bring romance or help you to connect with someone new on a deep level. It's important to remember that relationships are important to your happiness. Even when life gets busy, you need to make time for others and try to form meaningful connections.

Sunday 24th

It's likely to be a sociable Christmas Eve, especially if you're catching up with friends or joining in with festivities. If you're working today, try not to go into perfectionist mode. Focus on wrapping things up so that you don't miss out.

Monday 25th

Consider opening your doors to a wider social circle this Christmas Day, perhaps by helping out at a charity event. If you're at home, ensure that your Christmas is truly magical by embracing all of your family traditions.

Tuesday 26th

It could be an abrupt start to Boxing Day, especially if there's a major row or upset which prevents you from getting a good night's sleep. One way or another, things are likely to be noisy. Make time to put your feet up and take it easy later on.

Wednesday 27th

This is a busy time of year, particularly if you're working or being of service to others. Today's full moon calls out your compassionate and generous nature, especially if you're caring for others or looking after vulnerable people.

Thursday 28th

If you can, you might benefit from slowing things down and focusing on simple pleasures between Christmas and New Year. If you're in a noisy environment, it may all be too much for you now. Try not to lose your temper or feel resentful, and instead allow other people extra leeway.

Friday 29th

The moon returns to your star sign today, so this is your chance to shine. If you've made an effort to accommodate other people over the Christmas break, consider what you'd enjoy most in the last few days of 2023. A romantic date this evening might be a great choice.

Saturday 30th

Spend some time this weekend considering your hopes and dreams for 2024. Talk to those closest to you about their wishes and write down your intentions for the future. Be open to what the universe wants for you. Commit to expanding your world and doing more of what you love.

Sunday 31st

If you're not happy with your current job or situation, make a cosmic wish to move on and do things differently in the coming year. Look out for a new work opportunity that could arise in 2024. Celebrate with work colleagues this evening.

Leo

. . . .

PEOPLE WHO SHARE
YOUR SIGN

PEOPLE WHO
SHARE YOUR SIGN

. . . .

Leonians have studded the stage, ruled the roost and brought laughter and fun into people's lives for decades. Whether they choose to be actors, like Daniel Radcliffe, or sports stars, like Harry Kane, Leonians shine in the spotlight. Discover the courageous and sparkling stars who share your birthday and see if you can spot the similarities.

23rd July
Daniel Radcliffe (1989), Paul Wesley (1982), Kathryn Hahn (1973), Monica Lewinsky (1973), Marlon Wayans (1972), Philip Seymour Hoffman (1967), Slash (1965), Woody Harrelson (1961), Jo Brand (1957)

24th July
Turia Pitt (1987), Mara Wilson (1987), Elisabeth Moss (1982), Anna Paquin (1982), Rose Byrne (1979), Danny Dyer (1977), Jennifer Lopez (1969), Kristin Chenoweth (1968), Amelia Earhart (1897), Alexandre Dumas (1802)

25th July
Paulinho (1988), James Lafferty (1985), Shantel VanSanten (1985), D. B. Woodside (1969), Matt LeBlanc (1967), Iman (1955), Estelle Getty (1923), Rosalind Franklin (1920)

26th July

Stormzy (1993), Taylor Momsen (1993), Jacinda Ardern, Prime Minister of New Zealand (1980), Kate Beckinsale (1973), Jason Statham (1967), Sandra Bullock (1964), Helen Mirren (1945), Mick Jagger (1943), Stanley Kubrick (1928), Aldous Huxley (1894), Carl Jung (1875), George Bernard Shaw (1856)

27th July

Winnie Harlow (1994), Taylor Schilling (1984), Jonathan Rhys Meyers (1977), Tom Kerridge (1973), Maya Rudolph (1972), Nikolaj Coster-Waldau (1970), Triple H (1969), Julian McMahon (1968)

28th July

Harry Kane (1993), Cher Lloyd (1993), Soulja Boy (1990), John David Washington (1984), Alexis Tsipras, Greek Prime Minister (1974), Hugo Chávez, Venezuelan President (1954), Jacqueline Kennedy Onassis (1929)

29th July

Joey Essex (1990), Fernando Alonso (1981), Josh Radnor (1974), Wil Wheaton (1972), Sanjay Dutt (1959), Tim Gunn (1953), Geddy Lee (1953)

30th July

Joey King (1999), Yvonne Strahovski (1982), Jaime Pressly (1977), Hilary Swank (1974), Christine Taylor (1971), Christopher Nolan (1970), Simon Baker (1969), Terry Crews (1968), Lisa Kudrow (1963), Laurence Fishburne (1961), Arnold Schwarzenegger (1947), Henry Ford (1863)

31st July

Victoria Azarenka (1989), B. J. Novak (1979), Emilia Fox (1974), Antonio Conte (1969), Wesley Snipes (1962), Louis de Funès (1914)

1st August

Jack O'Connell (1990), Bastian Schweinsteiger (1984), Jason Momoa (1979), Ryoko Yonekura (1975), Coolio (1963), Yves Saint Laurent (1936), King Abdullah of Saudi Arabia (1924), Herman Melville (1819)

2nd August

Charli XCX (1992), Edward Furlong (1977), Sam Worthington (1976), Kevin Smith (1970), Mary-Louise Parker (1964), Wes Craven (1939), Peter O'Toole (1932), James Baldwin (1924)

3rd August

Karlie Kloss (1992), Charlotte Casiraghi (1986), Evangeline Lilly (1979), Tom Brady (1977), James Hetfield (1963), Martha Stewart (1941), Martin Sheen (1940), Terry Wogan (1938), Tony Bennett (1926)

4th August

Cole and Dylan Sprouse (1992), Meghan, Duchess of Sussex (1981), Anna Sui (1964), Barack Obama, U.S. President (1961), Billy Bob Thornton (1955), Louis Armstrong (1901), Queen Elizabeth, the Queen Mother (1900)

5th August

Olivia Holt (1997), Jesse Williams (1981), James Gunn (1966), Mark Strong (1963), Pete Burns (1959), Maureen McCormick (1956), Neil Armstrong (1930), Joseph Merrick (1862)

6th August

Charlotte McKinney (1993), Ferne McCann (1990), Robin van Persie (1983), Vera Farmiga (1973), Geri Halliwell (1972), Michelle Yeoh (1962), Barbara Windsor (1937), Andy Warhol (1928), Lucille Ball (1911), Alexander Fleming (1881)

7th August

Helen Flanagan (1990), Rick Genest (1985), Abbie Cornish (1982), Charlize Theron (1975), Michael Shannon (1974), David Duchovny (1960), Bruce Dickinson (1958), Wayne Knight (1955)

8th August

Shawn Mendes (1998), Princess Beatrice of York (1988), Roger Federer (1981), Meagan Good (1981), Chris Eubank (1966), The Edge (1961), Emiliano Zapata (1879)

9th August

Bill Skarsgård (1990), Anna Kendrick (1985), Audrey Tautou (1976), Gillian Anderson (1968), Eric Bana (1968), Whitney Houston (1963), Michael Kors (1959), Melanie Griffith (1957), Jean Piaget (1896)

10th August

Kylie Jenner (1997), Brenton Thwaites (1989), Devon Aoki (1982), JoAnna García (1979), Angie Harmon (1972), Justin Theroux (1971), Suzanne Collins (1962), Antonio Banderas (1960), Juan Manuel Santos, Colombian President (1951), Herbert Hoover, U.S. President (1874)

11th August

Alyson Stoner (1993), Jacqueline Fernandez (1985), Chris Hemsworth (1983), Anna Gunn (1968), Viola Davis (1965), Steve Wozniak (1950)

12th August

Cara Delevingne (1992), Mario Balotelli (1990), Tyson Fury (1988), François Hollande, French President (1954), George Soros (1930), Cantinflas (1911), Erwin Schrödinger (1887)

13th August

DeMarcus Cousins (1990), MØ (1988), Sebastian Stan (1982), Alan Shearer (1970), Debi Mazar (1964), John Slattery (1962), Fidel Castro, Prime Minister of Cuba (1926), Alfred Hitchcock (1899), Annie Oakley (1860)

14th August

Brianna Hildebrand (1996), Nick Grimshaw (1984), Mila Kunis (1983), Paddy McGuinness (1973), Halle Berry (1966), Emmanuelle Béart (1963), Magic Johnson (1959), Steve Martin (1945), Doc Holliday (1851)

15th August

Jennifer Lawrence (1990), Joe Jonas (1989), Ben Affleck (1972), Debra Messing (1968), Melinda Gates (1964), Alejandro González Iñárritu (1963), Anne, Princess Royal (1950)

16th August

Evanna Lynch (1991), Cam Gigandet (1982), Frankie Boyle (1972), Steve Carell (1962), Madonna (1958), Angela Bassett (1958), James Cameron (1954), Charles Bukowski (1920)

17th August

Taissa Farmiga (1994), Austin Butler (1991), Thierry Henry (1977), Donnie Wahlberg (1969), Helen McCrory (1968), Sean Penn (1960), Robert De Niro (1943), Mae West (1893)

18th August

Maia Mitchell (1993), Frances Bean Cobain (1992), G-Dragon (1988), Andy Samberg (1978), Edward Norton (1969), Christian Slater (1969), Patrick Swayze (1952), Robert Redford (1936)

19th August

Ethan Cutkosky (1999), Christina Perri (1986), Melissa Fumero (1982), Fat Joe (1970), Matthew Perry (1969), John Stamos (1963), Gerald McRaney (1947), Bill Clinton, U.S. President (1946), Gene Roddenberry (1921), Malcolm Forbes (1919), Coco Chanel (1883)

20th August

Demi Lovato (1992), Andrew Garfield (1983), Ben Barnes (1981), Amy Adams (1974), Misha Collins (1974), Fred Durst (1970), Joan Allen (1956), Robert Plant (1948)

21st August

Bo Burnham (1990), Hayden Panettiere (1989), Robert Lewandowski (1988), Usain Bolt (1986), Laura Haddock (1985), Carrie-Anne Moss (1967), Kim Cattrall (1956), Kenny Rogers (1938), Wilt Chamberlain (1936)

22nd August

James Corden (1978), Rodrigo Santoro (1975), Kristen Wiig (1973), Richard Armitage (1971), Adewale Akinnuoye-Agbaje (1967), Ty Burrell (1967), Honor Blackman (1925), Ray Bradbury (1920)

23rd August

Jeremy Lin (1988), Kobe Bryant (1978), Julian Casablancas (1978), Scott Caan (1976), Ray Park (1974), River Phoenix (1970), Rick Springfield (1949), Gene Kelly (1912)